BECOMING REAL:

A Journey Through Course and Self Discovery

By
SHIVANGI GUPTA

Becoming Real: A Journey Through Courage and Self-Discovery

ISBN: 978-93-5826-563-7

Contents

Preface

There comes a moment in every life when pretending feels heavier than honesty—when blending in feels more painful than standing apart. *Becoming Real: A Journey Through Courage and Self-Discovery* was born out of that moment.

For a long time, I tried to be who the world wanted me to be—polite, agreeable, effortless. But in chasing approval, I lost pieces of truth, of emotion, of myself. This book is my way of reclaiming them. It is a collection of reflections written from the quiet corners of thought, in moments of both chaos and calm. Each chapter captures fragments of growth, vulnerability, and courage—reminders that strength is not about perfection but about honesty.

I wrote this book for anyone who has ever felt misunderstood, unseen, or "too much." For those who have questioned their place in a world that demands conformity but secretly craves authenticity. For the hearts that feel deeply, the minds that think endlessly, and the souls that seek meaning beyond appearances.

These pages are not meant to instruct but to resonate—to remind you that you are not alone in your questions, your fears, or your search for truth. If even one sentence helps you breathe easier in your own skin, then this book has fulfilled its purpose.

Becoming Real is not about becoming perfect—it is about becoming whole. About peeling away layers of expectation until all that remains is you: raw, honest, and real.

Acknowledgement

I am deeply grateful to my family and friends, whose unwavering support and belief in me reminded me that being true to myself is always worth it. To everyone who challenged me, inspired me, or even doubted me—thank you for shaping the courage and resilience that fill these pages.

I also thank life itself for its lessons, both joyful and painful, for without them this book would not exist. Not For Everyone is a tribute to every soul who has ever felt different, misunderstood, or unheard—a celebration of authenticity, courage, and being unapologetically real.

Why I Wrote This Book

I wrote Becoming Real: A Journey Through Courage and Self-Discovery because there were moments when pretending felt easier than being honest, when fitting in seemed more critical than being myself. Every time I tried, I lost pieces of who I truly was. This book is my way of reclaiming that truth—a reminder that it's okay to be different, to feel deeply, and to live authentically.

Through these pages, I hope to reach anyone who feels unseen, unheard, or misunderstood, and tell them: you are enough, you are real, and you are worthy of living your truth. It is not about conforming; it is about embracing who you are, no matter what the world thinks.

Introduction

Life is full of paths, choices, and moments that challenge us to be honest with ourselves. This book is a reflection of those moments—the ones that teach us about courage, growth, and authenticity.

I wrote these pages to share experiences, thoughts, and reflections that matter deeply to me—and that I hope will resonate with anyone navigating life with curiosity, courage, and heart. Each chapter is a glimpse into moments of doubt, self-discovery, decisions, and emotions that shape who we are and who we strive to become.

This book is for those who think deeply, feel fully, and care about living a life true to themselves. It is not about perfection or rules. It is about learning, growing, and embracing the journey—even when it's challenging, confusing, or unconventional. As you read, I invite you to reflect, to pause, and to connect with your own thoughts and experiences. These stories are meant to inspire, guide, and encourage you to make choices that honor who you are, and to remind you that being authentic is one of life's most powerful journeys.

Section I

Awakening the Self: Understanding Who You Are

Theme:

Self-awareness, authenticity, inner truth, and the power of being "different.

Chapter 1

I'm Not Here to Be Understood

"In a world that tries to make you like everyone else, staying true to yourself is rebellion."

Sometimes, people look at you and whisper, "She's too much." Sometimes, they shake their heads and ask, "Why can't she just be simple?"

And you know what? They're right—only because you refuse to dilute yourself for their convenience.

Trying to be understood is exhausting. You spend hours explaining your emotions, justifying your choices, and defending your existence. And the sad truth? Most people never listen. They respond with what they expect, not what you need.

That's when you realize: you can't live for everyone. Trying to fit yourself into every expectation is a trap. True liberation begins when you accept that being "not for everyone" is not arrogance—it's fortitude. It's the deliberate choice to remain authentic in a world that constantly pressures conformity.

Some people will love the idea of you but not your reality. They will celebrate your energy but fear your silence. They will admire your achievements but shy away from your vulnerabilities. And that's okay. You don't need their validation.

Society often mislabels emotional depth as fragility, honesty as rudeness, and assertiveness as aggression. But here's the truth: feeling deeply is a strength. Speaking boldly is power. Setting boundaries is liberation.

I remember a day when I poured my heart out to someone who claimed to care, only to be dismissed. It hurt—deeply. But the pain taught me a lesson I will never forget: the people who truly belong in your life will accept every shade of you, including the chaos, the contradictions, and the raw emotion.

Being "not for everyone" is freedom. It's choosing yourself when everyone else questions your choices. It's speaking your truth even when your voice shakes. It's embracing your scars and owning your story. Life isn't about being universally palatable—it's about being unapologetically authentic.

You will lose people when you start being real. But you will also find yourself. And that's worth everything.

Every misalignment, every misunderstanding, every rejection is a reminder of your strength. Your energy isn't meant to fit every room, and your heart isn't meant to please every person. Protect it, honor it, and never compromise it.

Be unapologetic. Be audacious. Be tender and fierce at the same time. Be messy and perfectly imperfect. Be exactly who you are. Because some people won't understand you—and that's precisely why you're extraordinary.

Even in silence, even in solitude, even when no one notices—your truth matters. It is your power, your armor, and your liberation.

And that is the first step in learning that life isn't about making everyone comfortable—it's about making yourself unstoppable.

Chapter 2

The Strength in Being Broken

"Sometimes the cracks in us are where the light gets in."

There's a misconception people carry—that brokenness is weakness. That's when something inside you cracks; you are somehow less. I've learned the opposite. Brokenness is strength. Every fracture, every scar, every moment of pain is proof that you survived.

That you kept going when the world told you to stop. That you dared to feel when numbness would have been easier.

I remember sitting alone in my room, replaying moments that didn't go as I wanted, conversations that cut deeper than I expected, and mistakes that haunted me. My chest felt heavy, my thoughts loud, my heart unsure. And yet, through all that chaos, something extraordinary happened: I started noticing the little things. The lessons in silence. The growth in discomfort. The power in surviving my own storms.

Brokenness teaches you clarity. It teaches you to separate people and situations that truly matter from those that drain your energy. It teaches resilience—not the kind you read about in motivational quotes, but the real, raw resilience that forms when you look in the mirror and say, "I am still here. I am still me."

Not every day is triumphant. Not every victory is loud. Some battles are invisible, fought in quiet moments of reflection and introspection. The world rarely sees this kind of courage. And that's why it is precious. Those who recognize it are rare. Those who dismiss it are irrelevant.

Pain also teaches empathy. Once you've felt the sting of betrayal, the silence of misunderstanding, and the loneliness of being unseen, you start noticing the hidden battles others carry. You learn patience. You learn compassion. And most importantly, you learn to hold your own heart with care—not giving it away to people who aren't ready to honor it.

I've realized that life's most challenging moments shape the strongest people. That strength doesn't always look like confidence or bravado. Sometimes it seems like quiet acceptance. Sometimes it looks like saying no. Sometimes it looks like choosing yourself when everything around you screams that you should compromise.

Being broken isn't a flaw. It isn't failure. It is the foundation of authenticity, courage, and wisdom. And the beauty of it? When you embrace it, you become unstoppable. Your scars become maps—reminders of where you've been, and proof that you can survive wherever you go next. So, if you feel shattered today, remember this: strength doesn't come from avoiding pain. Strength comes from navigating it, learning from it, and rising despite it. Every tear, every heartbreak, every setback is shaping a version of you that is older, wiser, and unafraid. And here's the most essential truth: the people who matter won't leave you because of your cracks. They will stay. They will support. They will see your broken pieces and still call you extraordinary.

You are not broken to be fixed. You are broken to be stronger, wiser, and honest.

Chapter 3

Friends Who Stay, Friends Who Leave

"Those who leave make space for the ones who truly belong."

Friendship isn't always about constant laughter or shared secrets. Sometimes, friendship is about knowing who will show up when the world is quiet, when life isn't glamorous, when you're raw and vulnerable.

I've met people who loved my energy when I was happy, funny, and convenient.

But when life demanded depth, patience, and fundamental understanding, they disappeared. And I used to take it personally—thinking I wasn't enough, thinking I had done something wrong.

Then I realized: people leave. And sometimes, it's not about you at all. It's about them. Their fears, their insecurities, their inability to handle authenticity. And that's okay because those who are meant to stay will recognize your worth even in your most chaotic moments.

A true friend doesn't make your problems smaller by pretending they don't exist. They make your struggles lighter by standing with you. They don't just show up for the fun moments. They show up for the messy, complicated, emotional, and sometimes inconvenient parts of your life.

I remember a friend I considered inseparable. For months, I shared my thoughts, my dreams, my fears. I invested time, energy, and emotion. And then, one day, they vanished. No explanation, no closure, just absence. At first, I was heartbroken. But slowly, I realized: their absence was my lesson. My energy belongs to people who reciprocate, not people who take without giving.

Life has a way of testing relationships. The ones who endure are rare, but they are worth every ounce of effort. Learn to recognize who adds value and who drains energy. Learn to prioritize quality over quantity. It's not selfish—it's survival.

Friendship, like life, isn't perfect. People make mistakes, they falter, they hurt you. But the people who choose to stay, who return even after faltering, who respect your boundaries and emotions—those are the ones who matter. Hold them close. Treasure them. Protect them.

And those who leave? Let them go. Their departure is proof of life's selective nature, of the universe's subtle way of preparing space for the people who genuinely deserve to be part of your story. You will grieve, you will feel lost, you will question your worth. But remember this: the right friends amplify your energy. They support your growth. They celebrate your victories and honor your scars. They see your broken pieces and still call you extraordinary.

True friendship is rare. And when it comes, it's not loud or flashy—it's quiet, strong, and unwavering. It stays. Always.

Chapter 4

Silence Speaks Louder

"Those who leave make space for the ones who truly belong."

Not every emotion demands expression. Not every thought deserves a voice. In a world obsessed with constant communication, I have found the power of silence to be revolutionary. There were moments when saying nothing was the bravest act I could commit—moments when the room was loud but my mind needed quiet, when people demanded explanations but my soul needed space.

Silence became my teacher. It revealed truths I had overlooked, exposed patterns I ignored, and clarified my priorities when the noise of others clouded my judgment. In a generation addicted to likes, shares, and constant validation, silence is a rebellion. It's a sanctuary where clarity is born, where reflection is honored, and where self-understanding takes root.

I remember one evening, scrolling endlessly through messages and social media updates, feeling like I was losing myself in the external chaos. Everyone had opinions, everyone had judgments, and everyone demanded reactions. I chose silence. I chose reflection. I chose myself. And in that silence, I discovered resilience. I discovered perspective. I discovered the subtle strength of patience.

Sometimes, the most profound

conversations are held within the chambers of our own hearts. Sometimes, not responding is the loudest declaration of power. Learning when to speak and when to pause isn't a weakness—it's mastery of self. The world will attempt to confuse you, manipulate you, and provoke you. But your silence, when rooted in self-awareness, becomes a shield, a compass, and a declaration of autonomy.

The lesson I carry is simple yet revolutionary: respond, when necessary, react only when your inner voice demands it, and protect your energy fiercely. Silence is not surrender; it is strategy. And in the quiet, the extraordinary power of self-recognition blooms.

Chapter 5

Not All Battles Are Visible

"Strength isn't always seen; sometimes it's the courage to keep going unseen."

Some fights are silent, unseen, and unacknowledged. These are the battles that define who we become, yet rarely earn applause. The anxiety that keeps you awake at night, the fear that stops you from speaking, the heartbreak that reshapes your perception—these are battles fought in the invisible theater of the mind and heart.

I have carried wars within myself that no one witnessed. Moments when self-doubt whispered relentlessly, when insecurity disguised itself as logic, when loneliness wrapped around me like a cloak. And through these invisible battles, I discovered resilience that could not be measured by trophies or validation.

Life has a way of testing you quietly. It doesn't announce challenges in grandiose gestures. The most profound transformations often occur in solitude. Learning to navigate inner storms without applause or acknowledgment cultivates strength, patience, and self-trust.

The world rarely sees the courage in surviving your own mind. And that's why it is precious. Strength isn't always demonstrated through loud victories or visible achievements. Sometimes it's in the quiet persistence of continuing despite internal resistance, in the calm perseverance of facing each day fully aware of the weight you carry.

I remember a week when every interaction felt heavy. Misunderstandings at school, conflicts with friends, tension at home—all colliding in my head. No one noticed. No one offered guidance. No one intervened. And in that week, I realized: my strength wasn't measured by external validation. It was measured by endurance. By my ability to navigate the unseen storm with dignity and self-awareness.

Battles are not always recognized, but they shape you irrevocably. They mold empathy, resilience, and clarity. They teach you the value of boundaries, the importance of self-compassion, and the necessity of courage even when no one is watching.

Life doesn't hand out medals for surviving your inner chaos, but it rewards self-mastery in profound ways. When you emerge, scarred but intact, you carry knowledge, strength, and wisdom that no external acknowledgment can match.

The lesson is this: honor your internal battles and trust the process of invisible growth. Recognize that true courage is cultivated in the quiet, unseen moments of persistence, reflection, and self-belief. And always remember: your worth is not determined by what others see, but by the strength you nurture within.

Section II

The Power of Self-Choice

Theme:

Empowerment through boundaries, choices, self-prioritization, and resilience.

Chapter 6

Choosing Yourself

"The moment you choose yourself, the world may call it selfish — but your soul will finally call it peace."

I remember the first time I truly said no without guilt. It wasn't a dramatic, grand moment—no one applauded, no one understood. A friend asked me to bend my principles to help them. My instinct was to comply, to soften, to explain away my hesitation. But inside, a small voice whispered, "This is your line. Your energy. Your life. Protect it." Saying no was terrifying. My heart raced. My mind screamed rationalizations. I worried about judgment, about conflict, about losing someone I cared about. And yet, the moment I held firm, I felt something incredible—a rush of clarity, a spark of empowerment I had never experienced before. For the first time, I chose myself over convenience, comfort, or expectation.

Choosing yourself is not a selfish act. It is a declaration of self-worth. It is understanding that your energy is finite, your time is precious, and your emotions are not a public utility. For years, I allowed others' needs to take priority over my own. I showed up when it was inconvenient, I offered support when drained, and I silenced my own needs for approval. And every time, I felt the weight of resentment slowly creeping into my bones.

It was exhausting. One night, after a

particularly draining interaction with someone I thought was a friend, I sat on my bed, staring at the ceiling, questioning myself. "Why do I always bend? Why am I always responsible for everyone else's happiness?" I realized that in trying to please everyone, I had lost the most important person: myself.

Choosing yourself doesn't mean you stop caring for others. It means you stop sacrificing your core for temporary comfort. It means saying yes when your heart aligns and no when it doesn't. It means honoring your intuition, your needs, and your boundaries. It means recognizing that your life is yours to lead, not a service to everyone else's expectations.

I started applying this in small ways first. I declined invitations that drained me. I spoke up when I disagreed, even if it meant confrontation. I prioritized rest over productivity, authenticity over social approval, and self-care over overcommitment. Each choice felt radical at first, almost selfish. But the peace, clarity, and energy I gained were transformative.

Choosing yourself also means pursuing dreams even when no one believes in them. I had ambitions that seemed impossible, ideas that scared me, and a voice that trembled with
self-doubt. Society, friends, and even family questioned me: "Are you sure? Will it work? Isn't this too much?" Every no I heard from others felt heavy, but every yes I gave to myself felt like reclaiming a piece of my soul. It isn't easy. There are moments of guilt, waves of doubt, and the ever-present fear of loneliness. But I've discovered that self-alignment is worth every pang of discomfort. When you prioritize yourself, you attract people who respect your energy. You cultivate relationships that are reciprocal rather than draining. You build resilience against life's chaos, because your foundation is anchored in authenticity.

There's a misconception that choosing yourself makes you selfish, arrogant, or detached. But the truth is, only when you honor your own needs can you truly support, love, and understand others. A tree that is deprived of water cannot give shade. A heart that ignores its own voice cannot nurture another. Choosing yourself is not selfishness—it is survival, growth, and empowerment.

I remember a moment of confrontation with someone I loved. They accused me of being cold, distant, and uncaring. I listened, nodded, and then said, "I'm choosing me right now. And I hope one day, you understand that this is not against you. It's for me." Silence followed. Tension hung in the air. But I felt no regret. For the first time, I was free from the burden of constant
approval-seeking.

Choosing yourself requires courage, persistence, and self-reflection. It requires understanding your triggers, recognizing your limits, and honoring your values. It requires standing firm when the world pushes back. And each time you practice it, you grow stronger, wiser, and more aligned with your true self.

It also teaches a subtle but powerful lesson about relationships. People who truly belong in your life will honor your boundaries. They will respect your choices. They will celebrate your growth rather than fear it. And those who cannot—those who demand compromise, control, or energy that isn't yours to give—they are no longer yours to carry.

Life has taught me that choosing yourself is not a one-time act. It is a continuous practice. A daily declaration. A radical commitment to living authentically, unapologetically, and fully. And the reward? Peace, clarity, empowerment, and a life aligned with your deepest truth.

So, I continue to choose myself—every morning, every decision, every interaction. It isn't always easy, and it isn't always understood. But it is necessary. Because when you choose yourself, you reclaim your energy, your voice, and your life. And no external opinion can ever diminish that power.

Chapter 7

The Art of Letting Go

"Letting go isn't giving up; it's making room for what's meant for you."

Letting go is one of the hardest things you'll ever learn, not because it's painful, but because it forces you to confront the truth: not everything, not everyone, and not every situation is meant to stay in your life. For years, I clung to things that no longer served me—friendships that drained me, relationships that suffocated me, dreams that had shifted without me noticing. I thought holding on was a sign of loyalty, love, or perseverance. I was wrong.

I remember a friendship that had lasted nearly five years. On paper, it was perfect—laughter, shared secrets, long talks. But beneath the surface, I began to feel a constant weight, an emotional drain I could no longer ignore. Every interaction required effort that was never reciprocated, every conversation felt one-sided, and every call for help was met with excuses. I tried to rationalize, to make myself smaller so that the friendship could fit, to overlook the imbalance. And yet, my heart whispered something I couldn't ignore: "This is not for you anymore."

The day I finally stepped back, I felt panic. Fear. Guilt. I questioned myself endlessly: "Am I being unfair? Am I overreacting? Should I try harder?" But the more I resisted, the heavier the weight became. And then I realized: letting go isn't about giving up. It's about creating space for growth, for authenticity, and for people and opportunities who truly belong in your life.

Letting go is an act of courage. It is looking at what once mattered and acknowledging that it no longer serves your journey. It is facing discomfort and resisting the instinct to cling out of habit or fear. Letting go requires honesty—with yourself, with others, and with the world.

I still remember the quiet aftermath. No one called. No one explained. And initially, the silence felt like rejection, like failure. But slowly, I began to feel a sense of liberation I had never known. I had removed the weight of expectation, the energy drain, the constant emotional labor. I could breathe. I could think. I could finally live in alignment with myself.

Letting go also applies to expectations. Expectations of others, expectations of yourself, expectations of life. For years, I carried a blueprint of what life "should" look like—perfect grades, perfect friendships, perfect achievements. And every deviation felt like failure. It took immense self-reflection to understand that life rarely aligns with our plans. Clinging to unrealistic expectations only creates suffering. Letting go of them allows you to embrace reality, and in that space, growth becomes possible.

Another dimension of letting go is forgiving yourself. We cling to past mistakes, regrets, and moments of shame as if they define us. I held onto the memory of a betrayal—both inflicted and endured—for years. I blamed myself, dissected every choice, and carried guilt that was disproportionate to reality. When I finally forgave myself, I realized that letting go wasn't just about releasing others; it was about releasing myself from the prison of my own thoughts.

Freedom is born in letting go. Clarity emerges when you stop holding onto what no longer serves you. Strength is forged when you face fear, disappointment, and loss, and still choose to release the burden. And perhaps the most beautiful truth: letting go doesn't mean forgetting or devaluing your experiences. It means honoring your past, learning its lessons, and moving forward without carrying its weight.

I learned that life's flow is unpredictable. People will leave, circumstances will change, opportunities will vanish, and dreams will shift. The key is not to resist change but to embrace it. The moment you let go of what anchors you in the past, you create space for what is meant to be.

Letting go is a daily practice, not a one-time act. It is revisiting relationships, habits, and patterns regularly and asking: "Does this align with my growth? Does this honor my energy?" If the answer is no, the courage to release it becomes necessary. And each time you practice, you grow stronger, wiser, and more attuned to your own truth.

In the quiet moments after letting go, I discovered something profound: peace. Not loud, not flamboyant, not noticed by the world, but a quiet, unshakable peace that comes from knowing you chose yourself over attachment, authenticity over convenience, freedom over fear. And in that peace, life becomes lighter, clearer, and infinitely more meaningful.

Chapter 8

Imperfections Are Power

"It is courage that grows you up and makes you who you really are."

Perfection is a lie that society sells in glossy packages—the Instagram-worthy lives, the filtered smiles, the flawless routines. For years, I chased that lie, believing that if I polished myself enough, controlled my emotions enough, and hid every flaw, I would finally belong. I was exhausted. I was numb

. I was living a version of myself that wasn't real.

Then came the day I stopped pretending. It wasn't sudden. It wasn't dramatic. It began with a small, defiant thought: "What if I just... existed as I am?" The idea terrified me. Being imperfect, unpolished, and unapologetic felt dangerous. It went against everything I had been taught about success, acceptance, and love. But something inside me whispered that authenticity, not polish, was the real power.

I began experimenting. I let myself speak my mind without filtering every word. I allowed my emotions to show—anger, sadness, joy, and frustration alike. I stopped editing my reactions to fit the expectations of others. And I noticed something remarkable: the world didn't crumble.

People didn't leave. Life didn't punish me. In fact, something shifted.

Imperfections became my signature. The quirks, the contradictions, the scars, the mistakes—they were not flaws to hide but proof of life, courage, and experience. Each imperfection told a story, whispered lessons, and revealed layers of my character.

I remember a moment in school when I had made a huge mistake during a group project. Everyone expected me to apologize profusely, to cover up, to hide the error. But instead, I admitted it openly, took responsibility, and even laughed at my own misstep. The reaction was astonishing. People respected me more, not less. They saw authenticity, courage, and humility not weakness. That moment cemented a truth I now carry in every aspect of life: imperfection is power.

Our generation often battles the illusion of perfection. Social media bombards us with edited images, curated experiences, and the constant pressure to compare. But the more I embraced imperfection, the freer I became. The mistakes I once feared became lessons I cherished. The flaws I once hid became conversation starters, connection points, and bridges of understanding with others.

Imperfection fosters empathy. When you show your cracks, you allow others to show theirs. Vulnerability becomes a tool, not a weapon. It teaches you to accept yourself and others without judgment. And it reminds you that life is not about flawless execution, but meaningful experience.

I also learned to celebrate my contradictions—the fact that I can be both strong and tender, bold and hesitant, loud and quiet. Society often demands we fit neatly into one box, one label, one identity. But our power lies in our complexity. The contradictions, the gray areas, the messy corners of our being—they make us human, relatable, and unforgettable.

Another lesson emerged from embracing imperfection: the freedom to experiment. When you accept that you don't have to be perfect, you allow yourself to try, fail, and grow. You stop fearing mistakes and start pursuing bold choices. I began taking risks in my writing, friendships, and even daily life–because failure was no longer a reflection of my worth, but a tool for growth.

Imperfections are also a shield. People who try to bring you down often target your insecurities. But when you embrace your flaws, you disarm their power. You become unshakable, grounded in the knowledge that your worth is not determined by external validation or flawless execution, but by authenticity, courage, and resilience.

I think back to moments when I feared judgment–the awkward silences, the failed attempts, the stumbles in social interactions. Instead of hiding, I began owning them. I shared my laughter when I tripped over words, my thoughts when they seemed strange, my quirks when others raised eyebrows. Each act of authenticity strengthened me, built my confidence, and inspired connections that were real, not performative.

The most profound lesson I've learned: imperfection is magnetic. It draws people who are real, who are curious, who are willing to connect on a deeper level. It pushes away superficiality, performative admiration, and empty approval. And in that natural filtration, life becomes richer, relationships deeper, and growth inevitable.

Imperfection is also a form of self-love. By accepting yourself as you are—with scars, mistakes, contradictions, and quirks—you nurture inner peace. You stop battling yourself, stop pretending to be someone you're not, and start living fully. And that authenticity becomes contagious. People around you feel safer, freer, and more inspired to embrace their own truths.

I've come to believe that our generation's true power lies in embracing imperfection unapologetically. In a world obsessed with flawless images and curated lives, being raw, vulnerable, and honest is revolutionary. It takes courage to admit weakness, joy to embrace flaws, and wisdom to recognize that imperfection is the foundation of authenticity.

So, I carry my scars proudly, laugh at my mistakes, and celebrate the messy, complex, beautiful human that I am. Because in a world that often demands conformity, the real victory is in authenticity. The real strength is in vulnerability. And the real magic is in knowing that imperfections are not shortcomings—they are power.

Chapter 9

Fear Isn't Weakness

"Fear is proof that you're alive and daring to grow."

Fear. It is a shadow that follows you silently, sometimes barely noticeable, sometimes overwhelming, wrapping itself around your thoughts, your heart, your every decision. For a long time, I believed fear was a flaw—proof that I wasn't brave enough, strong enough, or capable enough. I thought fear meant hesitation, failure, and weakness.

But the truth, the hard-earned truth, is that fear is not weakness. Fear is a compass. Fear is a teacher. Fear is proof that you are alive, conscious, and capable of growth.

I remember the first time I faced a fear that consumed me. I had spent months writing a story that was personal, raw, and vulnerable. Every word was a fragment of my soul, every paragraph an unfiltered reflection of my emotions. Sharing it felt terrifying. My mind screamed: "What if people hate it? What if they mock you? What if this changes how they see you?" The fear was suffocating. I wanted to hide it, delete it, pretend it didn't exist.

And yet, I didn't. I took a deep breath, pressed "send," and released it into the world. The response was... overwhelming. Not in the way I expected. Some people didn't understand it, some criticized it, and some ignored it. But others resonated with it, wrote back to me, thanked me, and shared their own stories. I realized in that moment that fear is not a sign to retreat; it is a signal that something important is at stake—something worth confronting, something worth risking.

Fear is not a stop sign. It is a guidepost, showing you the edges of your comfort zone, revealing the areas where growth waits. Every time I feel fear, I ask myself: "What is this teaching me?
What am I avoiding? What opportunity lies beyond this moment of discomfort?" Fear has pushed me to speak when I wanted to stay silent, to act when I wanted to wait, to love when I wanted to protect myself with walls.

I've also learned that fear comes in many forms. Sometimes it is loud—an anxiety that roars in your chest, a worry that keeps you awake at night. Sometimes it is quiet—a subtle hesitation, a whisper of doubt, a small voice urging caution. Both forms are equally powerful. Both deserve recognition. And both can be harnessed as a source of strength if approached with courage and reflection.

I recall a particular incident at school. I had been asked to speak in front of the entire class—a task that terrified me. My palms sweated, my heart raced, and my mind faltered. I wanted to run, hide, make an excuse, anything to avoid the fear. But I stood there anyway. I spoke, stumbled over words, laughed nervously, and finished. And in that moment, I discovered the paradox of fear: the act of facing it often makes it smaller, while avoiding it allows it to grow. Fear is also deeply personal. The things that scare you are often connected to your values, your vulnerabilities, and your aspirations. I fear rejection because I care deeply about connection. I fear failure because I want my efforts to mean something. I fear judgment because I value authenticity. And acknowledging these fears has allowed me to understand myself more deeply. Fear isn't a flaw; it's a mirror reflecting what matters to you most.

What most people don't realize is that fear can be liberating if approached correctly. It forces you to examine your limits, to challenge assumptions, and to redefine what is possible. Every time I step into fear, I step closer to growth. Every time I act despite fear, I reclaim power that I once surrendered to doubt.

I have learned to treat fear like a friend—not one that comforts me, but one that guides me. I listen, I respect, and I act anyway. Fear warns, but it doesn't dictate. It signals boundaries, but it doesn't confine. It challenges, but it doesn't imprison.

There have been moments when fear threatened to paralyze me completely. Times when I wanted to give up on a project, a friendship, or a dream because the stakes felt too high. But every time I faced the fear, even in small ways, I discovered resilience I didn't know existed. I discovered a voice I thought was too quiet. I discovered courage that had been hidden behind layers of doubt and hesitation.

Fear also teaches patience. Sometimes the right action is not immediate confrontation, but careful preparation, reflection, and timing. I've learned that rushing through fear rarely leads to growth. Observing it, understanding it, and planning within its presence often yields the most profound results.

One of the most important lessons I've internalized is that courage is not the absence of fear. Courage is action despite fear. It is persistence when the mind screams to stop. It is commitment when the heart trembles. It is the quiet voice that whispers, "I may be scared, but I will do it anyway."

Fear is also a measure of potential. The things that scare you often indicate the areas where you are capable of extraordinary growth. My writing terrified me, public speaking terrified me, emotional vulnerability terrified me—

and in facing each, I discovered a depth of self and an impact on others that would have been impossible without the fear.

I remember writing a particularly vulnerable piece about heartbreak. Fear told me to hide it. Fear told me I would be judged. Fear told me I wasn't ready. But I published it anyway. Within days, messages poured in from strangers who had experienced the same pain. They felt seen. They felt understood. They felt less alone. And I realized: fear is not a barrier; it is a bridge to courage, connection, and transformation.

So, I embrace fear now, not as an enemy, but as a guide. I feel it, acknowledge it, and then act. I step forward trembling, but I step forward nonetheless. Because the truth I have discovered is this: the presence of fear is not weakness—the decision to move despite it is the strongest thing you can do.

Every step taken despite fear strengthens the mind, sharpens the heart, and expands the soul. Every risk embraced despite fear teaches resilience, patience, and authenticity. Every time fear is acknowledged, confronted, and acted upon, life reveals its depth, beauty, and possibilities.

And for anyone reading this, I want you to carry this truth: fear is not your enemy. Fear is your guide, your teacher, and your proof that you are alive. Facing fear doesn't make you fearless. Facing fear makes you unstoppable. Facing fear makes you real. Facing fear makes you extraordinary.

Chapter 10

Boundaries Are Liberation

"Saying no is not cruelty; it's self-respect in its purest form."

Boundaries. The word itself feels both protective and confrontational. For a long time, I didn't understand their power. I thought boundaries were walls—barriers built to keep others out, selfish defenses, or signs of detachment. But as I grew, I realized that boundaries are not walls.

They are the markers of self-respect, the signals of energy, and the very definition of personal freedom.

I spent years being available, accommodating, and bending to fit the expectations of others. I said yes when I wanted to say no. I stayed late, sacrificed sleep, and pushed my own needs aside to ensure everyone else's comfort. I believed this was kindness. I believed this was love. I believed this was what made me "good." But slowly, I began to feel the weight of exhaustion, resentment, and invisibility pressing down on me.

It started with small realizations. A friend constantly demanded my attention but rarely asked how I was. A family member imposed expectations without consideration for my limits. A teacher criticized my choices without acknowledging my effort. I gave and gave, until one day I realized I had nothing left to give—not because I was incapable, but because I hadn't taken care of my own needs.

Boundaries aren't selfish. They are self-preservation. They are the recognition that your energy is finite, your time is precious, and your emotions are not public utilities. Setting boundaries is an act of courage—a declaration that you will no longer compromise your well-being to appease others. It is the first step in reclaiming autonomy over your life.

I remember the first time I set a real boundary. A friend wanted me to help them with something that I had no time or energy for. My instinct was to say yes, to avoid conflict, to be "good" and "helpful." But I paused. I looked at my schedule, my mental state, and my priorities. And then, I said no. The reaction was immediate. There was surprise, subtle disappointment, even a hint of anger. And yet, I felt a surge of relief. I had not betrayed anyone. I had not abandoned anyone. I had simply honored myself. That small act of saying no became a lesson I carried forward: boundaries protect your energy, they teach respect, and they liberate you.

Boundaries apply everywhere–in friendships, family, romance, work, and even within ourselves. They are the limits you set on time, energy, emotions, and expectations. They teach others how to treat you, what is acceptable, and what is not. And perhaps most importantly, they teach you how to value yourself.

I've had to enforce boundaries with people who didn't like them. There were friends who felt offended, family who felt challenged, and colleagues who felt rejected. And yet, the more I practiced, the more I understood: those who truly respect you will honor your boundaries; those who cannot, are not yours to carry.

Setting boundaries is also about emotional self-defense. It is about protecting yourself from manipulation, undue stress, and draining relationships. It is saying, "I will not sacrifice my peace for the comfort of someone else's ego." It is claiming the right to prioritize your own life, without guilt, shame, or apology.

I remember a time when I allowed someone to continuously disrespect me under the guise of friendship. I smiled, nodded, and tolerated behavior that made me uncomfortable, believing that it was loyalty. Over time, the resentment built, and I felt trapped, exhausted, and invisible. Only when I established clear boundaries—speaking up, walking away, and refusing to compromise my peace—did I feel the liberation I had been missing.

Boundaries are not static. They evolve with your growth, experience, and changing priorities. What was acceptable yesterday may no longer serve you today. Recognizing this fluidity is key to maintaining self-respect and personal freedom. Revisiting, reinforcing, and renegotiating boundaries is not weakness—it is wisdom.

Boundaries also teach clarity in relationships. People who respect them are aligned with your values, intentions, and energy. People who resist them reveal themselves for what they are. Boundaries are a filter—a natural selection process that cultivates meaningful, reciprocal, and nourishing connections.

One of the most important lessons I've learned is that boundaries are freedom, not limitation. They are not about isolating yourself or avoiding responsibility. They are about creating a safe space for your energy, focus, and growth. They allow you to say yes to what matters and no to what doesn't. They grant permission to live authentically, unapologetically, and fully.

The liberation of boundaries is subtle but profound. It is the peace in knowing that your choices are your own. It is the relief of protecting your energy without guilt. It is the confidence that comes from understanding your limits and enforcing them consistently.

And it is the power that emerges when you prioritize yourself without fear of judgment. I have come to embrace boundaries as sacred. They are a daily practice, a personal commitment, and a mark of self-love. Every time I enforce them, I reclaim a piece of my life. Every time I honor them, I strengthen my resilience. Every time I communicate them clearly, I inspire respect—both for myself and from others.

In a world that constantly demands your time, energy, and attention, boundaries are revolutionary. They remind us that we are not obliged to carry the weight of others' expectations. They teach us that self-respect is non-negotiable. They prove that liberation is not found in permission from others, but in the courage to say yes to yourself.

So, I continue to set boundaries—bold, clear, unwavering. It isn't always comfortable. Some people are offended, some push back, some leave. And that's okay. Because in the end, boundaries are not about keeping people out—they are about keeping yourself in. Keeping your energy intact. Keeping your integrity unshaken. Keeping your freedom alive.

Boundaries are not walls. Boundaries are liberation. And for anyone seeking empowerment, clarity, and peace, they are the most radical act of love you can offer yourself.

Section III

The Strength Within

Theme:

Vulnerability, patience, courage, and emotional maturity.

Chapter 11

The Strength in Vulnerability

"The truest measure of self-discovery is not in the moment you find your real self, but in the sustained, defiant choice to keep living as them, every single day."

For a long time, I believed that vulnerability was a sign of weakness. I thought showing emotions, admitting mistakes, or revealing fears would make me fragile, exposed, and easy to hurt. I built walls around my heart, disguised my feelings behind humor or indifference, and convinced myself that strength meant invulnerability. But life has a way of teaching lessons that no amount of stubbornness can avoid.

I learned the hard way that true strength lives in vulnerability. It began with a personal failure—a friendship I had trusted, a project I had poured my soul into, a dream that slipped from my fingers despite endless effort. My instinct was to hide, to retreat, to pretend that nothing had happened. I wanted to appear strong, composed, and unaffected. But the weight of pretending became unbearable. It manifested as sleepless nights, anxiety, and an almost physical heaviness in my chest.

One evening, I called my closest friend. My voice trembled. My words stumbled. I admitted my fears, my doubts, my pain. And instead of judgment or dismissal, I was met with understanding, empathy, and connection. In that moment, I realized that vulnerability was not weakness—it was courage, intimacy, and power.

Vulnerability allows us to connect authentically with others. It bridges the gap between isolation and empathy, loneliness and understanding, fear and resilience. By showing our true selves—our struggles, our uncertainties, our imperfections—we invite others to do the same. And in that shared humanity, bonds are forged stronger than any pretense or facade could ever create.

I began practicing vulnerability in small ways. I admitted when I didn't know something. I shared my opinions honestly, even when controversial. I expressed gratitude freely. I allowed myself to cry, laugh, and feel deeply without restraint. Each act felt risky at first, but each act also brought relief, clarity, and a sense of liberation.

There were times I was hurt, misunderstood, or rejected because of vulnerability. It stung, but I learned that vulnerability is not a guarantee of safety—it is a commitment to authenticity. And authenticity is worth the risk, every single time.

Vulnerability is also a tool for self-discovery. By confronting our fears, insecurities, and limitations, we uncover truths about ourselves we might otherwise ignore. I discovered strengths I didn't know I possessed, values I was willing to fight for, and passions I had long buried under self-protective armor.

Being vulnerable does not mean oversharing or losing boundaries. It means choosing when, how, and with whom to open your heart. It is a conscious act of trust, courage, and wisdom. When balanced with boundaries, vulnerability becomes a superpower—a way to live fully, love deeply, and connect meaningfully.

I remember an experience during a group activity where I had to present my personal story in front of strangers. My hands shook. My voice quivered. My heart raced. But as I shared, I noticed eyes softening, heads nodding, and people leaning in. My fear turned into connection, my insecurity into empathy, and my trembling words into power. That day, I understood: showing your true self is more influential than hiding behind a mask of perfection.

Vulnerability also teaches resilience. Each time you expose your heart, you discover the ability to recover, adapt, and grow. Life will challenge, disappoint, and hurt you, but vulnerability allows you to feel deeply, learn profoundly, and live fully. It transforms fear into courage, loneliness into connection, and weakness into strength.

The greatest lesson I've learned: vulnerability is not a weakness to be ashamed of, nor a risk to avoid. It is a choice—a conscious decision to be real, raw, and present. It is the pathway to authenticity, empathy, and deep fulfillment.

By embracing vulnerability, I reclaimed my voice, my heart, and my life. I stopped hiding. I stopped performing. I started existing fully, unapologetically, and courageously. And in that existence, I discovered freedom, power, and joy unlike anything I had known before.

Chapter 12

The Power of Patience

"The truest courage is not in running the race, but in stopping to face the mirror you have avoided."

Patience has always felt like a quiet, almost invisible virtue—one that society rarely celebrates but life often demands. For years, I struggled with impatience, rushing through experiences, relationships, and decisions as if speed alone could guarantee success or happiness. I wanted results, validation, and closure immediately, forgetting that the richest lessons are often hidden in the slow, unremarkable moments we try to skip.

I first learned the meaning of true patience during a creative project that mattered deeply to me. I had invested months of time, energy, and heart into writing, editing, and refining a piece I considered my best work. Yet, the process tested me in ways I had not anticipated. Feedback was slow, mistakes were made, and progress felt frustratingly incremental. My mind screamed, "Why isn't it done yet? Why am I still waiting?"

But through the discomfort, I discovered a truth: patience is not passive. It is not idle waiting. It is an active engagement with time, effort, and growth. Patience is a quiet strength that allows you to persevere, learn, and evolve while trusting that results will arrive in their own time.

I started practicing patience intentionally. I began breaking down large goals into small, manageable steps, celebrating progress instead of fixating solely on outcomes. I reminded myself that life rarely unfolds according to plan, and that the journey–with all its struggles, setbacks, and uncertainties–often teaches more than the destination.

One day, I reflected on a friendship that had weathered years of misunderstanding and distance. I could have given up, walked away, and sought comfort elsewhere. Instead, I chose patience–listening, forgiving, and giving space for growth. Over time, that friendship evolved, strengthened, and blossomed in ways I could not have forced or rushed. Patience, I realized, is an investment in relationships, allowing them to develop organically rather than being dictated by urgency or expectation.

Patience is equally vital in personal

growth. For years, I criticized myself for not being "enough"—smart enough, confident enough, creative enough. I wanted change overnight, as if growth were a linear, immediate process. But self-discovery and transformation unfold slowly. Every small decision, every reflection, every setback contributes to a larger picture that patience alone allows you to see clearly.

I remember a time when I failed a personal goal repeatedly. My instinct was to abandon it, to label myself incapable, and to give up entirely. But patience taught me to approach the challenge differently—to learn from mistakes, adjust strategies, and persevere with quiet resilience. Over time, I not only achieved the goal but learned far more from the process than the outcome itself. Patience had become my ally, my teacher, and my shield against frustration.

Another lesson patience offers is perspective. When we rush, we often react impulsively, make mistakes, and overlook details that matter. But when we cultivate patience, we gain clarity. We see situations more objectively, understand others more empathetically, and make choices aligned with long-term growth rather than fleeting impulses.

Patience also requires trust—trust in yourself, in others, and in life's timing. It asks you to believe that challenges will resolve, efforts will be recognized, and opportunities will arrive when they are meant to. This trust is not passive optimism; it is a conscious acknowledgment that life unfolds with a rhythm beyond immediate comprehension, and that forcing outcomes often undermines their true potential.

I learned patience in the most unexpected places—waiting for opportunities, waiting for answers, waiting for forgiveness, waiting for recognition. Each instance tested my ability to surrender control while staying engaged. And each time, I discovered that waiting is not weakness; it is strength in disguise. It builds resilience, deepens understanding, and strengthens character.

Patience is also intertwined with self-compassion. When we rush ourselves, we invite stress, anxiety, and self-criticism. When we allow ourselves the time to grow, to heal, and to learn, we cultivate kindness toward ourselves—recognizing that progress is rarely linear and that mistakes are essential to growth.

I recall a difficult period in my life when everything seemed delayed—my goals, my friendships, my sense of clarity. I felt frustrated, anxious, and impatient. But through quiet reflection, journaling, and small daily actions, I began to embrace the rhythm of patience. I stopped comparing my journey to others, stopped expecting immediate results, and began focusing on consistent effort. Slowly, things shifted. Opportunities emerged, relationships strengthened, and personal growth accelerated—all because I had allowed patience to guide my path.

The most profound lesson patience offers is this: the journey matters more than the destination. Every delay, every setback, every uncomfortable moment carries lessons, insights, and growth. Rushing through life may bring temporary satisfaction, but patience cultivates depth, understanding, and fulfillment.

For anyone learning to embrace patience, I would say this: notice the small moments. Celebrate incremental progress. Trust the timing of life. Listen to your instincts while allowing space for growth. Understand that your efforts are never wasted, even if results are delayed. And remember, patience is not passive waiting; it is active, intentional, and transformative.

By embracing patience, I have discovered resilience, clarity, and strength. I have learned to navigate life's uncertainties with grace, to honor my own pace, and to trust in the unfolding of my journey. Patience is not merely a virtue—it is a superpower, a form of quiet courage that transforms every aspect of life.

And now, when life tests me with delays, setbacks, or uncertainty, I no longer panic. I breathe, I observe, I act with intention, and I wait with faith. Because the power of patience lies not in avoiding challenges, but in embracing the journey fully, one deliberate step at a time.

Chapter 13

The Courage to Speak Up

"You must unbecome who you are not before you can truly become who you are."

Silence can feel safe. It can feel protective. It can feel like control. For years, I relied on silence–holding back thoughts, hiding opinions, and pretending that my voice didn't matter. I believed that keeping quiet would prevent conflict, avoid judgment, and ensure I fit in. But life has a way of teaching that silence is not always protection; often, it is surrender.

The first time I truly understood the courage of speaking up was in class. A topic was being discussed, and everyone around me had strong opinions. My heart raced. My mind spun. I wanted to stay quiet, blend in, and avoid drawing attention. But something inside me pushed forward—a whisper that my perspective mattered, that my thoughts deserved to be heard.

When I spoke, my voice trembled. I stumbled over words. Some people disagreed. Some laughed. Some didn't understand. But a few nodded. A few smiled. A few stayed curious. And in that moment, I realized something powerful: speaking up is not about being perfect—it's about being present, honest, and courageous.

Our generation often struggles with this. We live in a world that encourages conformity, fear of judgment, and the comfort of blending in. But growth, connection, and authenticity thrive when voices are raised, when ideas are shared, and when truths are spoken—even if imperfectly.

Speaking up doesn't mean shouting or dominating conversations. It means asserting your ideas, expressing your feelings, and standing for what you believe, even when it's uncomfortable. It's choosing presence over passivity, honesty over avoidance, and courage over fear.

I remember a moment when a close friend was being treated unfairly, and I hesitated to intervene. My fear of conflict kept me quiet for a while. But the longer I stayed silent, the heavier the guilt became. Eventually, I spoke—gently, firmly, and with clarity. The result wasn't perfect resolution, but it was real impact. The friend felt supported, the situation shifted, and I discovered that courage is not the absence of fear but the choice to act despite it.

Speaking up is also a practice of self-respect. It communicates boundaries, values, and integrity. When we refuse to voice our needs, opinions, and feelings, we allow others to shape our lives without consent. Each time we assert ourselves, we reclaim ownership over our experiences.

I've learned that speaking up requires preparation—not perfection. It requires reflection, awareness, and empathy. I think before I speak, I consider the impact, but I never silence my truth to placate others. Over time, this balance builds confidence, credibility, and respect.

Another lesson I discovered is that speaking up often inspires others. Vulnerability, honesty, and courage are contagious. When one person voices what others feel but fear, a ripple effect begins. People who feel alone or overlooked realize they are not invisible. Conversations deepen. Connections strengthen. And communities become more authentic.

The Courage to Speak Up

There were moments when speaking up had consequences. Disagreement, tension, and even conflict arose. But I realized that the discomfort of truth is preferable to the long-term cost of silence. Speaking up doesn't guarantee agreement or approval—it guarantees authenticity and self-respect.

Courage in speech also extends to personal expression—sharing art, writing, ideas, and emotions. I've shared my thoughts through stories, poems, and reflections, fearing judgment yet choosing honesty. Each time, the act of expression became more liberating than the fear of criticism. It taught me that words, when spoken with integrity, have power—power to heal, connect, and transform.

Sometimes, speaking up requires standing alone. Opinions, beliefs, or truths may not be popular. People may resist, mock, or misunderstand. But courage is about choosing authenticity over approval, honesty over comfort, and impact over ease.

The strongest voices are often those that dare to speak when silence seems safer.

I remember a school debate where my perspective clashed with the majority. My heart raced, palms sweated, and my voice shook. Yet, I presented my argument with clarity, honesty, and confidence. I didn't win the debate, but I won something greater—self-respect, awareness, and courage. Speaking up, even imperfectly, had transformed me.

The courage to speak up also nurtures inner clarity. When you express your thoughts and feelings, you understand them better. You process emotions, articulate values, and discover priorities. Silence may feel safe, but it often clouds understanding and delays growth. Speaking up illuminates truth—both to others and to yourself.

I've learned to pair courage with empathy. Speaking up is not about imposing opinions or attacking others. It is about honesty, integrity, and constructive expression. When done with awareness, speaking up resolve's conflicts, inspires dialogue, and nurtures mutual respect.

The most profound lesson I've learned: your voice matters. Your perspective matters. Your truth matters. Speaking up is not just about influencing others; it is about affirming your own existence, honoring your values, and living authentically. Silence may seem easier, but courage is transformative.

So, I continue to speak up—in classrooms, in friendships, in writing, and in life. I stumble, falter, and hesitate at times, but I never retreat into silence when truth calls. Because the courage to speak up is not just a skill; it is a declaration: I exist. I matter. I am not invisible.

Chapter 14

The Strength in Letting Go

"Authenticity is not a plea for acceptance; it is a boundary that says, 'This is me. Take it or leave it.'"

Letting go is one of the hardest lessons life asks us to learn. For a long time, I believed that holding on meant strength—clinging to relationships, past experiences, failures, and even grudges. I thought if I let go, I would be weak, defeated, or unfaithful to memories

and promises.
But slowly, I discovered that true strength is not in holding on; it is in the courage to release, to accept, and to move forward.

The first time I truly understood this was with a friendship that had once felt unshakable. Over time, misunderstandings, repeated disappointments, and unspoken resentment accumulated. I kept trying—texting, meeting, explaining, forgiving—because I believed loyalty meant persistence, no matter the cost. Yet, every attempt left me drained, anxious, and bitter. One evening, I reflected and realized something: loyalty is not about holding on at the expense of your peace. Loyalty is about honoring connections that are mutual, respectful, and nurturing. I made the decision to let go—not out of anger, but out of self-respect and clarity. The initial release was painful, full of grief and doubt, but it brought an unexpected relief: space for growth, understanding, and new possibilities.

Letting go is not just about relationships. It is about thoughts, habits, fears, and expectations that weigh us down. I have let go of perfectionism, of self-criticism, and of unrealistic standards. I have let go of fears that kept me from expressing my creativity, speaking my truth, or pursuing opportunities. Each release felt like shedding chains, revealing a lighter, freer version of myself.

There is a misconception that letting go is passive. That it means giving up or abandoning responsibility. But letting go is active, deliberate, and courageous. It requires awareness, honesty, and acceptance. It is a conscious choice to stop fighting what cannot be changed and to focus energy where it matters.

I remember a particular challenge during my writing journey. I had poured months into a piece I loved, but no matter how much I revised, it didn't feel right. My instinct was to force it, perfect it endlessly, or abandon it entirely. But I took a step back, allowed myself to release the attachment, and approached it later with fresh perspective. The work transformed—not because I forced it, but because I let go and created space for clarity, creativity, and insight.

Letting go also requires forgiveness—of others, and of ourselves. Holding onto anger, resentment, or regret binds us to the past, preventing growth. I have forgiven people who hurt me, not because they deserved it, but because I deserved peace. I have forgiven myself for mistakes, knowing that guilt and regret cannot rewrite the past but can poison the present.

Forgiveness is the ultimate act of letting go, and it is profoundly liberating.

I have learned that letting go is deeply personal. It is not about what others think or expect. It is about what your heart, mind, and soul need to thrive. Some things are meant to stay; others are meant to leave. Recognizing the difference requires honesty, courage, and trust in life's rhythm.

There is also a strength in letting go of control. I used to believe that if I controlled everything—outcomes, expectations, people's reactions—I could avoid disappointment. But life has a way of reminding us that control is often an illusion. Letting go of the need to control allows space for growth, spontaneity, and unexpected opportunities. It teaches patience, trust, and humility.

I remember a moment when I had to let go of a dream that I had cherished for years. I had worked tirelessly, hoped endlessly, and imagined countless scenarios of success. But circumstances, timing, and reality forced me to release it. Initially, I felt grief, frustration, and failure. But in that release, I discovered resilience, perspective, and new paths I hadn't considered. Letting go didn't end my journey—it redirected it.

Letting go also creates space for love, joy, and creativity. When we release toxic relationships, negative emotions, and limiting beliefs, we open our hearts to experiences that truly matter. We discover clarity in priorities, freedom in choices, and peace in acceptance. Life feels lighter, fuller, and more vibrant.

One of the most important lessons I've learned is that letting go is not a one-time act. It is a continuous practice. We let go daily—of stress, of expectations, of judgments, of regrets. Each act strengthens resilience, deepens self-awareness, and nurtures emotional maturity.

The courage to let go transforms fear into freedom, grief into growth, and pain into insight. It allows us to step into life fully—with open hearts, clear minds, and unburdened souls. I have learned that holding on may feel secure, but releasing creates liberation, possibility, and power.

So, I practice letting go of what no longer

serves me, what drains my energy, and what limits my growth. It is not easy. It is not quick. It is not without emotion. But every time I release, I discover strength I didn't know existed, courage I didn't know I had, and freedom I didn't know I deserved.

Letting go is an act of love—for life, for others, and for yourself. And in that love, in that release, in that conscious surrender, we find the truest strength of all.

Chapter 15

Embracing Change

"The greatest discovery you will ever make is the quiet power of your own company."

Change is inevitable. Yet, for years, I treated it as a threat. A storm to endure. A disruption to avoid. A loss of control. I resisted it, clung to the familiar, and feared the unknown. But life, in its relentless rhythm, taught me that embracing change is not only necessary—it is transformative.

The first time I truly understood this was when my daily routine was disrupted unexpectedly. A friend moved away, a project I loved ended abruptly, and plans I had meticulously crafted fell apart. My instinct was panic. I wanted to cling, recreate, and control. But in the silence of that moment, I realized: resistance amplifies fear; acceptance fosters growth.

Change is a teacher, often disguised as discomfort. It challenges our habits, beliefs, and perspectives. It forces us to confront ourselves, question our priorities, and adapt. I have learned that when we resist change, we waste energy fighting life's natural flow. When we embrace it, we unlock opportunities, insight, and strength we never imagined.

I remember a time when I had to switch schools unexpectedly. Initially, I felt anger, fear, and sadness. I resisted new routines, unfamiliar faces, and altered friendships. But slowly, I decided to approach the situation differently—to explore, connect, and learn. That decision transformed an intimidating change into an empowering experience. I discovered resilience, new perspectives, and the courage to thrive outside my comfort zone.

Embracing change also requires trust—in yourself, in others, and in life. We cannot control every outcome, but we can choose our response. Each change, each challenge, each shift offers a chance to grow stronger, wiser, and more adaptable.

One of the most profound lessons I've learned is that change reveals character. When situations shift, relationships evolve, or plans collapse, our reactions define us. Do we resist, blame, and fear? Or do we adapt, learn, and move forward? Change strips away pretenses, exposing both vulnerability and strength.

I once faced a creative project that demanded completely new skills—skills I didn't think I had. My first attempts failed. I doubted myself, questioned my abilities, and considered giving up. But embracing change meant learning, experimenting, and persevering. Over time, I not only succeeded, but I also discovered potential within myself I hadn't recognized. Change had become a catalyst for growth.

Embracing change requires flexibility. Life rarely unfolds according to plan. People leave, opportunities shift, and circumstances transform. By remaining rigid, we trap ourselves in frustration, disappointment, and stagnation. By staying flexible, we adapt, evolve, and find new paths that align with our goals and values.

There is also courage in embracing emotional change—acknowledging shifting feelings, evolving relationships, and transforming priorities. Change may bring loss, grief, or discomfort. But it also brings clarity, freedom, and understanding. Accepting this emotional flow allows us to move through life with greater awareness, compassion, and resilience.

I learned to embrace change in my personal growth journey. I had to let go of limiting beliefs, old fears, and expectations that no longer served me. The process was uncomfortable and at times frightening. But each release opened space for creativity, confidence, and self-discovery. I realized that holding onto the past often prevents us from becoming who we are meant to be.

Change also teaches patience. Growth, transformation, and progress unfold gradually. Impatience leads to frustration, regret, or forcing outcomes prematurely. Patience, combined with adaptability, allows us to navigate change gracefully, learning lessons fully and appreciating the journey.

I recall a period when a close relationship shifted unexpectedly. I felt hurt, confused, and uncertain. My first instinct was to resist—to cling, to argue, to demand things remain the same. But I chose to embrace the change—to understand, reflect, and adapt. The relationship evolved, and while it was different, it became deeper, more honest, and more aligned with mutual respect.

Embracing change also fosters self-reliance. When we navigate new experiences, challenges, or environments, we discover capabilities we didn't know existed. We learn to trust our judgment, instincts, and adaptability. Each successful adaptation strengthens confidence and resilience, proving that we are stronger than our fears.

Change is not always comfortable. It can be messy, unpredictable, and emotional. But within that discomfort lies opportunity. The more we resist, the more we suffer. The more we accept, the more we grow. Life unfolds in layers, and embracing change allows us to experience each layer fully, with curiosity and courage.

One of the most empowering

realizations I've had is that change is never permanent in one form. It shifts, evolves, and cycles. Embracing change doesn't mean surrendering to chaos; it means participating actively in the process, learning, adapting, and shaping your path while flowing with life.

By embracing change, I have discovered freedom, strength, and clarity. I have learned to navigate uncertainty with courage, to trust my journey, and to find opportunity in every ending. Change, once feared, has become a teacher, a catalyst, and a friend.

So now, when life shifts unexpectedly, I don't panic. I don't resist. I observe, adapt, and act with intention. I understand that every change, whether big or small, is an invitation to grow, to learn, and to live fully. Embracing change is not just a matter of survival; it is a transformation, liberation, and the truest expression of courage.

Section IV

Growth, Change & Transformation

Theme:

Evolution, adaptability, healing, and celebrating progress.

Chapter 16

The Beauty of Small Wins

"The journey to 'real' doesn't end; it simply unfolds, one brave, imperfect step at a time."

For years, I had this belief that life only mattered if the milestones were grand—awards, recognition, success, or achievements that everyone could see and admire. I thought that anything small was insignificant, barely worth celebrating, and certainly not enough to make a difference. But life has a way of teaching that the small wins, the invisible victories, the quiet accomplishments, are often the most transformative.

It all began with something seemingly trivial. I had been procrastinating on a project—a small writing piece I had promised myself I would finish by the end of the week. For days, I kept delaying, distracted by other "more important" tasks, telling myself, "It's not that big a deal. I'll finish it later." But that small, postponed task lingered in my mind, quietly creating stress, guilt, and tension.

One evening, I decided to sit down and complete it—no distractions, no excuses. The process was slow and imperfect. My sentences stumbled at first; my ideas didn't flow naturally. But after hours of focus and persistence, I finished. The sense of accomplishment, though small, was overwhelming. That night, I realized: small victories build momentum, confidence, and resilience in ways that big achievements often cannot.

I began noticing these small wins everywhere. Waking up early consistently, completing daily tasks on time, helping someone without expecting recognition, finishing a chapter of writing, or speaking my opinion in a difficult conversation—every act, however minor it seemed, mattered. Each one was a step forward, a confirmation that I was capable, growing, and moving toward my goals.

Celebrating small wins isn't about arrogance or self-indulgence. It's about awareness, gratitude, and perspective. When we acknowledge the little achievements, we cultivate a mindset of growth and positivity. I started journaling these wins daily—not the big awards or recognition, but the personal victories that reflected effort, courage, and persistence.

Over time, this simple practice shifted my entire perspective on success.

One lesson I learned the hard way is that small wins often precede big changes. I remember struggling with my confidence during a public speaking exercise at school. Initially, I could barely make eye contact with the audience. My hands shook; my voice trembled. But I set small, achievable goals: speak clearly for five seconds without fear, maintain eye contact with one person, practice gestures slowly. Each tiny victory, however minor, built my confidence. After weeks of these small steps, I was able to present an entire speech with poise and clarity—something that once seemed impossible. The cumulative effect of these small wins was extraordinary.

Small wins also teach patience. Life does not always reward instant success. Big achievements often require persistent effort over long periods. By focusing on the small, daily victories, I learned to value progress rather than immediate results. This approach nurtured resilience, as I began to understand that every step forward, no matter how small, counts.

There is also a moral embedded in small wins–humility. Celebrating minor victories reminds us that life is not just about the spotlight, recognition, or applause. Sometimes, the most meaningful progress happens quietly, unnoticed by others. Learning to appreciate these moments fosters self-awareness and gratitude.

I recall a moment when I volunteered to organize a small school event. It wasn't a huge competition or an award-winning performance–it was just a local gathering for a few students and teachers. Initially, I thought it wouldn't matter. But every small task I completed–coordinating decorations, arranging schedules, and solving minor problems–built a sense of accomplishment that I had never anticipated. On the day of the event, everything ran smoothly, and I felt pride, not because of recognition, but because I had contributed meaningfully. That day, I understood that impact is often in the details, and significance does not always shout to be heard.

Small wins also strengthen relationships. Celebrating little acts of kindness, moments of support, or shared experiences creates deeper connections. I learned to acknowledge when friends accomplished something small—like helping someone, sharing a difficult thought, or being consistent in their efforts. These recognitions, though minor, strengthened bonds and encouraged mutual support. Life, I realized, is made up of countless small gestures that matter far more than grand, dramatic acts.

Another profound lesson from small wins is that they build confidence gradually. I was always hesitant to voice my opinions in groups, fearing judgment or rejection. But starting with small contributions—a comment here, a question there—I began to feel my voice mattered. Each positive reinforcement, each nod, each acknowledgment—small wins—encouraged me to speak more boldly over time. This accumulation of confidence eventually transformed my personality, making me more assertive, authentic, and self-assured.

Small wins also teach reflection. When I pause to consider what I have accomplished daily, even the tiniest things, I notice patterns of growth. I see areas where I am consistent, where I struggle, and where I am improving. These reflections guide my decisions, priorities, and actions. Life is less overwhelming when I focus on tangible, achievable victories rather than being paralyzed by the enormity of long-term goals.

Interestingly, small wins cultivate resilience in failure. Every tiny success acts as a buffer against discouragement. When larger challenges arise—rejection, disappointment, or setbacks—recalling past small victories reminds me of my capacity to overcome. It reinforces a mindset of persistence, reminding me that every effort counts, even if it doesn't immediately succeed.

I've also realized that small win's nurture creativity. By breaking larger goals into smaller, achievable tasks, I allow my mind the freedom to explore, experiment, and innovate without fear of failure. Each small accomplishment provides feedback and insight, creating a continuous cycle of learning and growth. Creativity, like confidence, thrives in an environment where small wins are acknowledged and celebrated.

Even self-love is strengthened through small wins. Recognizing your daily efforts—whether it's choosing healthy habits, setting boundaries, or investing in self-care—validates your worth and efforts. I learned to celebrate these personal victories without guilt, understanding that growth is incremental, and every effort deserves recognition.

The beauty of small wins lies in their cumulative power. Over time, tiny steps transform into profound change. I have seen habits solidify, confidence grow, relationships deepen, and resilience strengthen—all because small, consistent efforts were acknowledged and embraced. Life, I realized, is a mosaic of these small wins, and each one contributes to the masterpiece of our journey.

So, I made a conscious choice: to notice, celebrate, and value small victories every day. I remind myself that even when life feels overwhelming, even when success seems distant, every step forward matters. Every completed task, every honest conversation, every effort counts. And slowly, these small wins add up to something extraordinary—a life lived fully, intentionally, and with purpose.

The moral is clear: do not underestimate the power of small wins. They shape character, nurture confidence, and create lasting impact. Life is rarely defined by a single achievement—it is defined by the accumulation of countless small victories, each quietly building the person you are meant to become.

Chapter 17

The Courage to Fail

"Failure is a compass pointing you toward your truest path."

Failure is something we fear from the moment we first try. I used to believe that failure defined who we are—a mark of weakness, incompetence, or inadequacy. For a long time, I avoided risks, skipped challenges, and settled for comfort because I feared failing. But life has an ironic way of teaching: the courage to fail is the gateway to growth, confidence, and transformation.

I remember my first major experience with failure vividly. I had spent weeks preparing for a school competition—a debate that I was confident I could win. I researched, practiced, and memorized arguments. The night before, I felt excitement mixed with nervous energy. I believed I had done everything perfectly. But when I stepped onto the stage, my mind went blank. Words stumbled, sentences broke, and my confidence shattered. I didn't just lose; I flopped completely.

At first, I was devastated. I replayed the experience over and over, scolding myself for not being "good enough." I avoided facing my peers, avoided the next school event, and considered giving up on debating entirely. I thought this failure defined me. But gradually, I realized that failure was not the enemy—fear of failing was.

Failure teaches lessons that success cannot. It exposes weaknesses, highlights gaps, and forces introspection. After that debate, I reflected deeply. I identified areas to improve—my preparation, my public speaking techniques, and my ability to stay calm under pressure. I also realized something more important: even though I failed publicly, my value and potential were not diminished.

The courage to fail means daring to try despite uncertainty. It is the willingness to step into the unknown, to risk embarrassment, rejection, or disappointment. Every successful person I admire, from authors to athletes, has faced countless failures. What sets them apart is not perfection, but persistence and the mindset that failure is feedback, not defeat.

I learned to reframe failure in my daily life. Instead of seeing a low grade, a missed opportunity, or a rejected idea as a disaster, I began to view them as lessons. Each "failure" became a map—showing what worked, what didn't, and what could be improved. This perspective transformed fear into curiosity, and hesitation into action.

One of the most profound lessons of failure is humility. When we fail, we recognize that we are human—imperfect, learning, and evolving. I remember struggling with a creative project I had written for school. I had spent hours crafting the story, perfecting dialogues, and imagining every detail. When my teacher returned the feedback, pointing out flaws and gaps I hadn't noticed, I felt crushed. But then I realized that this feedback, this exposure of my mistakes, was an opportunity to grow. Humility in failure allows us to accept criticism, adapt, and become stronger.

Failure also cultivates resilience. I recall an instance where a personal friendship didn't go as I hoped. I felt hurt, misunderstood, and rejected. It felt like a failure in connection, a test of my ability to communicate and trust. But reflecting on it taught me patience, empathy, and the importance of boundaries. Each time we fail, we build emotional muscles, preparing us for future challenges.

I've learned that courage and failure are inseparable. Taking risks, pursuing dreams, and expressing ideas all carry the possibility of failure. But the alternative—never trying—guarantees stagnation. I once hesitated to submit a poem to a competition, fearing judgment and rejection. Yet, I sent it anyway. It didn't win. But the act of submitting, despite fear, was a victory in itself. I felt empowered, brave, and capable. That day, I realized that the act of trying, even when failure is likely, is itself a triumph.

Failure also strengthens self-awareness. When we fail, we confront our limitations, strengths, and desires. I began to notice patterns in my mistakes—procrastination, overthinking, fear of confrontation—and learned to address them. Failure revealed my blind spots and guided me toward personal growth.

One of the most challenging aspects of failure is the fear of judgment. Society often equates failure with incompetence, and this pressure can paralyze us. But I discovered that judgment is temporary; lessons last forever. The courage to fail means prioritizing growth over approval, self-expression over criticism, and authenticity over perfection.

Failure also nurtures creativity and innovation. In moments of failure, I discovered alternative solutions, new perspectives, and untested ideas. When one approach didn't work, I explored another. The willingness to fail opened doors to creativity that I never would have explored if I had only sought "safe" successes.

I remember working on a group project that initially fell apart. Our ideas clashed, our planning was messy, and it seemed impossible to succeed. Failure was imminent. But instead of giving up, we analyzed mistakes, reorganized, and tried new strategies. The result was better than expected—not because we avoided failure, but because we learned from it and adapted. Failure had guided us to a stronger outcome.

There is also courage in sharing your failures. I began writing about my mistakes, insecurities, and struggles. I worried about judgment and ridicule. Yet, sharing openly created connection, understanding, and empathy. Others resonated with my experiences, realizing that failure is universal and that courage is contagious.

Most importantly, failure teaches perseverance. Life rarely rewards instant success. Goals require repeated effort, trial, and error. Every failure is a stepping stone toward mastery. I learned that persistence, fueled by lessons from failure, is more valuable than effortless victories.

The moral is clear: do not fear failure.

Embrace it. Learn from it. Grow because of it. Courage is not the absence of failure, but the choice to keep moving forward despite it. Life is not defined by perfection, but by resilience, adaptability, and the bravery to try again and again.

I now approach challenges with a mindset that blends hope and realism. I understand that setbacks will come, mistakes will happen, and failures will be inevitable. But these are not endpoints. They are invitations—to reflect, adapt, and rise stronger. Each failure is a rehearsal for success, a lesson in courage, and a testament to persistence.

So, I take risks. I try new things. I voice opinions. I submit my writing. I explore unknown paths. I fail sometimes. I fall sometimes. But I always rise. And in that rising, I discover the most valuable truth: failure is not my enemy—it is my teacher, guide, and ally in the journey of becoming.

Chapter 18

The Strength of Self-Love

"Loving yourself fiercely is the first rebellion against a world that doubts you."

For the longest time, I measured my worth through the eyes of others. I sought validation in grades, approval in smiles, recognition in compliments, and identity in how others perceived me. I criticized my every mistake, compared myself relentlessly, and dismissed my efforts because they seemed small or inadequate. I thought self-love was selfish, vain, or unnecessary. But life, as always, taught me otherwise.

I remember sitting alone one rainy evening, feeling exhausted from trying to please everyone around me—teachers, friends, even family. Every achievement felt hollow if it wasn't acknowledged by others. Every mistake felt monumental because I internalized criticism without mercy. I asked myself a simple question: "When will I acknowledge myself?"

Self-love is not arrogance. It is not ego. It is the quiet, powerful acknowledgment that you matter, your efforts matter, and your existence is valuable. It is the recognition that you are deserving of care, patience, and respect—from yourself first, and then from others.

I began to practice self-love in small, intentional ways. I started journaling—not to impress, not to compare, but to honor my thoughts, feelings, and reflections. I wrote about my daily victories, however small, and celebrated my efforts. I forgave myself for mistakes, knowing they did not define me. I set boundaries, learning to say no without guilt, protecting my energy from unnecessary demands. Each act of self-love felt revolutionary, a reclamation of my own value.

One of the earliest lessons I learned is that self-love is an act of courage. In a world that constantly judges, compares, and criticizes, claiming your worth is defiant. I remember raising my voice in a class discussion, not because I wanted attention, but because I had a perspective to share. Fear whispered that I would be judged, laughed at, or dismissed. But I silenced it with self-belief, and the moment I spoke, I realized: respecting myself is far more powerful than fearing external judgment.

Self-love also manifests in forgiveness–forgiving others and, most importantly, yourself. I had carried guilt for

years over minor mistakes, missed opportunities, and moments of perceived failure. That guilt weighed heavily, limiting my confidence and happiness. But embracing
self-love taught me that forgiveness is liberation. Letting go of self-blame and resentment made room for growth, joy, and clarity.

I recall a time when I struggled with a creative project. I compared my work relentlessly with peers, feeling inadequate. Instead of abandoning the project or succumbing to self-criticism, I decided to nurture my efforts with patience and encouragement. I allowed myself to make mistakes, learn, and improve without judgment. The final outcome was not perfect, but it reflected my authenticity and growth—a product of self-love.

Self-love strengthens resilience. When we value ourselves, setbacks and criticism no longer define us. I have faced disappointments in friendships, academic challenges, and personal goals. Each time, the ability to ground myself in self-worth allowed me to persevere, adapt, and learn without losing confidence. Self-love became my anchor amidst life's uncertainties.

Another profound aspect of self-love is authenticity. Loving yourself allows you to express your true thoughts, emotions, and desires without fear. I realized that hiding parts of myself to gain approval or avoid conflict only led to frustration, anxiety, and disconnection. When I started honoring my feelings and expressing them honestly, relationships deepened, creativity flourished, and life felt more meaningful.

Self-love also cultivates empathy. By acknowledging and nurturing my own emotions, I became better at understanding the feelings of others. Compassion flowed naturally, not as a duty, but as an authentic response. I could support, encourage, and connect with others more genuinely because

I had first learned to support, encourage, and connect with myself.

I remember a moment when a friend was struggling silently. My instinct was to offer advice, solutions, or judgments. But self-love taught me the value of presence—listening without interference, validating feelings without dismissing them, and offering support without sacrificing my own boundaries. The experience highlighted that self-love is not isolation; it is the foundation for meaningful connections.

There is also courage in prioritizing yourself. Saying no, choosing solitude, or taking time for self-care can feel uncomfortable in a world that glorifies busyness and self-sacrifice. But self-love reminds us that our needs, dreams, and well-being are valid, and honoring them is necessary for personal growth. I started allocating time for writing, reflection, and creative expression, and discovered that nurturing myself amplified my capacity to give to others.

Self-love encourages continuous growth. When we value ourselves, we invest in our development—mentally, emotionally, and spiritually. I began reading, journaling, reflecting, and practicing mindfulness. Each act reinforced my self-worth and built a foundation of confidence that could weather challenges, criticism, and uncertainty.

One of the most difficult lessons of self-love is letting go of toxic influences. I realized that not all relationships, habits, or environments supported my growth. Loving myself required courage to release negativity, distance from judgmental people, and the choice to prioritize my own well-being over external expectations. That release, though challenging, created space for healthier relationships, creativity, and personal fulfillment.

Self-love is also about celebrating individuality. Society often pressures us to conform, compare, and compete. I noticed my tendency to judge myself harshly for being different—in interests, thoughts, or style. But embracing self-love meant honoring my uniqueness, appreciating my quirks, and taking pride in my individuality. This acceptance cultivated confidence, authenticity, and joy.

I have learned that self-love is not static. It is a continuous practice, requiring reflection, patience, and adaptation. Some days, I succeed effortlessly; other days, I falter, doubt, or feel insecure. The key is to return to self-love consistently, gently, and without judgment. Each effort reinforces resilience, growth, and authenticity.

There is immense power in self-love. It transforms fear into confidence, criticism into reflection, and doubt into clarity. It allows us to take risks, express ourselves, and navigate life with courage. I now approach challenges, relationships, and creative endeavors with a mindset rooted in self-worth. Because when you love yourself, you no longer seek validation externally—you become your own source of strength and guidance.

So, I practice self-love daily—through reflection, care, expression, and forgiveness. I celebrate my achievements, however small. I honor my emotions, acknowledge my needs, and nurture my growth. Life is not perfect, but self-love makes it purposeful, resilient, and vibrant.

The moral is clear: strength is born from self-love. When you value yourself, embrace your uniqueness, and honor your journey, you gain the courage, resilience, and clarity to navigate life boldly, authentically, and unapologetically.

Chapter 19

The Power of Listening

"Courage isn't the first step; it's the silent commitment to keep walking even when the map you held was always wrong."

For the longest time, I underestimated listening. I thought speaking, being heard, or making an impression mattered more than understanding others. I wanted to express, argue, explain, and assert. I believed that to connect, I had to talk, perform, or impress.

But life, as it often does, showed me a truth I couldn't ignore: listening is the bridge to understanding, empathy, and meaningful connection.

I remember one afternoon in school when a friend approached me, visibly upset. My instinct was to offer advice, cheer them up, or tell them what they should do. I started speaking immediately, trying to "fix" the problem. But they didn't respond, their eyes distant, their posture tense. That's when I paused. I realized I hadn't really listened–I had only prepared my response. In that moment, I consciously stopped speaking and simply let them share. I focused entirely on their words, tone, and expressions. I didn't interrupt. I didn't judge. I just listened.

And something remarkable happened. Slowly, their posture relaxed. Their voice steadied. They shared thoughts they hadn't told anyone before. By simply listening, I created a space for them to be heard, understood, and supported. That moment changed my perspective forever: listening is a gift, for both the speaker and the listener.

Listening is not passive. It requires presence, attention, and empathy. True listening demands that we quiet our minds, resist the urge to respond immediately, and focus fully on the other person's experience. I have practiced this in friendships, family, and creative collaborations, and each time, the depth of understanding I gained was remarkable.

There is also a moral in listening: humility. When we listen genuinely, we acknowledge that our perspective is not the only one. We recognize that others have experiences, feelings, and insights that are equally valid. I recall a disagreement with a classmate over a project. I was convinced I was right, ready to argue my case. But I paused and listened to their reasoning. In that moment, I discovered nuances I hadn't considered, which not only improved the project but also strengthened our mutual respect. Listening taught me that wisdom often comes from understanding, not dominating a conversation.

Listening builds empathy. When we hear someone's story without judgment, we step into their world, even briefly. I remember helping a junior student navigate anxiety about exams. Initially, I offered tips and suggestions, but they seemed distant, unresponsive. I then simply asked them to tell me how they felt. I listened intently as they described sleepless nights, racing thoughts, and fears of failure. I didn't interrupt. I didn't correct. I just acknowledged. That act of listening provided comfort, trust, and validation. Empathy flourishes in the silence of listening.

Listening also strengthens relationships. In our fast-paced, digital age, most conversations are about responding, debating, or impressing. Rarely do we stop to genuinely listen. I noticed that my closest friendships deepened when I made the conscious effort to listen more than I spoke. Celebrating someone's triumphs, understanding their struggles, or simply sharing their silence creates bonds that words alone cannot form.

There is power in listening to ourselves as well. Self-awareness grows when we pause, reflect, and listen inwardly. I journal, meditate, and observe my thoughts and feelings. By truly listening to myself, I identify desires, fears, and motivations I might otherwise overlook. This practice allows me to make decisions aligned with my values rather than reacting impulsively or seeking external approval.

Listening requires patience. People often communicate in layers—words, tone, body language, and emotion. It takes time to unravel meaning, understand intention, and sense unspoken truths. I recall a heated discussion with a friend that could have ended in anger. Instead of interrupting, I listened carefully, deciphering underlying emotions and fears. By the end, not only did we resolve the conflict, but our bond was stronger than before. Patience in listening transforms misunderstandings into connection.

Active listening is also a form of respect. It signals to others that their thoughts, feelings, and experiences matter. I have noticed that when I listen attentively, people open up more, share more honestly, and feel valued. Respect and trust flourish naturally when one listens without judgment, interruption, or pretense.

Listening nurtures creativity and learning. I have discovered ideas, perspectives, and solutions simply by listening—in classrooms, collaborative projects, or casual conversations.

Sometimes, a simple story shared by someone else sparks inspiration, provides clarity, or shifts my thinking. By listening, we absorb knowledge that cannot be found in books alone.

There is courage in listening, especially when what we hear is uncomfortable. Difficult truths, criticism, or differing perspectives can trigger defensiveness. But true listening requires openness and bravery. I remember receiving critical feedback on my writing. My first instinct was to defend myself. Instead, I paused, listened carefully, and reflected on the feedback. This approach improved my work and strengthened my confidence. Courage in listening transforms challenge into growth.

I also learned that listening is an act of love. When we are present, empathetic, and attentive, we communicate care without words. I have seen relationships mend, conflicts resolve, and trust deepen through simple, genuine listening. Love often speaks louder through understanding than through grand gestures or constant advice.

Listening is not limited to conversations. Nature, experiences, and life itself speak if we pay attention. I have spent hours sitting quietly, observing the rain, the wind, and the rhythm of life around me. These moments of listening cultivate mindfulness, gratitude, and awareness. Life becomes richer when we learn to listen—not just to words, but to experiences, emotions, and silence.

Self-reflection through listening has also taught me patience and resilience. By paying attention to my own growth, mistakes, and successes, I have learned to navigate life with intention. I notice patterns, recognize areas for improvement, and celebrate progress. Listening inwardly complements listening outwardly, creating harmony, clarity, and self-understanding.

Ultimately, the power of listening is transformational. It bridges gaps between people, nurtures empathy, strengthens bonds, encourages growth, and cultivates wisdom. I now approach every conversation with a conscious intent to listen first, understand second, and speak thoughtfully only when necessary. I realize that words spoken without understanding often create conflict, while silence paired with listening fosters connection.

So, I practice listening daily—to friends, family, teachers, peers, and myself. I pause to hear what is not said, observe subtleties, and reflect on experiences. Listening is not passive; it is active, intentional, and courageous. It teaches humility, compassion, and insight. It transforms relationships, enriches learning, and nurtures self-awareness.

The moral is clear: listening is a superpower. It requires patience, courage, and empathy, but its rewards are immeasurable. By listening deeply, we connect more authentically, understand more fully, and live more meaningfully. In a world obsessed with speaking, being heard, and performing, the true strength lies in pausing, observing, and listening with intention.

Chapter 20

The Journey Within

"The truest conversations you will ever have are the silent ones you finally allow yourself to have with your own soul."

For years, I chased the external–grades, achievements, recognition, friendships, validation. I thought life's meaning was measured by accomplishments others could see. But slowly, painfully, and beautifully, I realized that the most profound journey is the one within–exploring thoughts, emotions, desires, fears, and values.

I remember a period when I felt completely lost. Everything I did felt hollow, even successes that once thrilled me. Smiles, compliments, and accolades seemed superficial. I was constantly seeking answers outside myself, in people's approval, trends, or achievements. Nothing satisfied me. One quiet evening, I asked a question I had avoided for years: "Who am I really, beyond what everyone else sees or expects?"

The journey within is not easy. It is uncomfortable, demanding, and sometimes frightening. It requires honesty, introspection, and courage. I began to journal, meditate, and reflect on my choices, thoughts, and emotions. I confronted fears I had buried, insecurities I had ignored, and patterns that limited me. For the first time, I faced myself without distraction, denial, or pretense.

I realized that true growth cannot happen without understanding oneself.

External achievements are fleeting; they do not define identity or purpose. By exploring my inner world, I discovered strengths I hadn't recognized, passions I had suppressed, and desires I had dismissed as unrealistic. The journey within revealed clarity that no external success could provide.

Self-awareness is the first gift of the journey within. I began noticing patterns in my behavior—moments of fear, procrastination, self-doubt, and comparison. I identified triggers for stress, sadness, and frustration. I also recognized my resilience, creativity, and courage. Awareness alone empowered me to make intentional changes, rather than reacting impulsively or letting life dictate my path.

The journey within also taught me emotional intelligence. I learned to identify, understand, and manage my emotions rather than suppress or ignore them. I reflected on moments of anger, disappointment, or jealousy, asking: "Why do I feel this? What does it teach me?" By listening to my emotions without judgment, I transformed them from obstacles into guides, helping me navigate life with clarity and balance.

I remember a time when a friendship ended unexpectedly. My initial reaction was sadness, anger, and confusion. But through reflection, I realized the experience was a mirror, revealing my expectations, boundaries, and values. The journey within helped me process emotions, release resentment, and gain insight. I didn't just move on; I grew stronger, wiser, and more compassionate.

Inner exploration fosters creativity. By observing thoughts and feelings, I discovered ideas, stories, and solutions that had previously been hidden. I began to write with authenticity, express opinions boldly, and create without fear. The journey within unlocked creativity not by external validation, but by self-connection.

The path inward also nurtures resilience. Life is unpredictable, filled with challenges, failures, and setbacks. By understanding my inner landscape—my fears, strengths, and limitations—I learned to navigate uncertainty with confidence. I became aware that resilience is not just surviving external challenges, but mastering inner turbulence.

Patience is another lesson of the journey within. Self-discovery cannot be rushed. Understanding patterns, processing emotions, and uncovering desires requires time. I learned to sit with discomfort, reflect without judgment, and allow growth to unfold gradually. Each day, each reflection, each insight became a step forward, even when progress felt slow.

Self-love is deeply intertwined with the journey within. By recognizing my worth, embracing my flaws, and nurturing my strengths, I cultivated self-respect and compassion. I realized that self-love is not a destination but a practice—nurtured through reflection, awareness, and care.

The journey within also illuminates values and priorities. In moments of decision, I now pause to ask: "Does this align with who I am and what I value?" Understanding internal motivations clarifies choices, strengthens integrity, and ensures actions resonate with authenticity rather than external pressure.

I recall a personal challenge when I had to choose between a comfortable path and one that aligned with my passions. Initially, fear and doubt clouded my judgment. But reflecting inward, listening to my intuition, and evaluating my desires helped me make a choice that felt courageous, authentic, and fulfilling. The journey within provided clarity that external opinions or societal expectations could not.

Inner exploration also fosters empathy. By understanding my own emotions, struggles, and growth, I became more attuned to the experiences of others. I could listen more deeply, respond more thoughtfully, and connect more genuinely. Compassion, I realized, starts within—only then can it extend outward.

The journey within requires honesty—with oneself, with feelings, and with thoughts. It demands that we face uncomfortable truths, admit mistakes, and question assumptions. I have faced insecurities, unrealistic expectations, and self-imposed limitations. Confronting them was painful, but necessary. Each revelation provided a new layer of understanding and freedom.

One of the most profound lessons I've learned is that the journey within is ongoing. There is no final destination, no endpoint. Growth is continuous, and self-understanding deepens over time. Every experience, challenge, and reflection adds richness, clarity, and resilience. Life becomes less chaotic, not because external circumstances change, but because we navigate them with awareness, intention, and inner strength.

The journey within also enhances mindfulness. I began noticing moments of gratitude, joy, and beauty that previously passed unnoticed. By being present with my thoughts and feelings, I cultivated appreciation for life's subtleties. Each moment became meaningful, every experience an opportunity to learn, reflect, and grow.

I realized that the journey within shapes external reality. Decisions, actions, relationships, and achievements become aligned with values, desires, and authenticity. Life becomes purposeful, intentional, and fulfilling when guided by inner clarity.

So, I continue the journey within—through journaling, meditation, reflection, and

self-observation. I embrace discomfort, confront fears, and celebrate insights. I listen to my intuition, honor my emotions, and nurture my growth. Life is not perfect, but self-connection makes it meaningful, empowering, and vibrant.

The moral is clear: true strength, clarity, and fulfillment come from the journey within. By exploring thoughts, emotions, and values, by cultivating self-awareness, and by listening to us inner voice, we gain the tools to navigate life with courage, purpose, and authenticity. The external world may be chaotic, unpredictable, and demanding, but inner understanding creates resilience, clarity, and freedom.

The journey within is the greatest adventure, the most profound challenge, and the most rewarding path. And in this journey, we discover not only who we are but who we are capable of becoming.

Section V
Living Authentically

Theme:

Forgiveness, self-belief, purpose, and living your truth.

Chapter 21

Embracing Change

"The lie that felt comfortable is a heavier burden than the hard-won truth that cuts deep."

Change has always scared me. Even as a child, the thought of leaving behind the familiar, stepping into uncertainty, or venturing beyond comfort filled me with anxiety. I clung to routines, people, and habits, believing that stability was safety. But life, in its quiet persistence, taught me an undeniable truth: change is inevitable, necessary, and transformative.

I remember the first time I truly confronted change. My best friend moved to another city, a shift that felt like losing a part of myself. At first, I resisted—I avoided calls, replayed memories, and hoped things would somehow remain the same. But slowly, I realized that clinging only prolonged pain. I had two choices: resist the change or embrace it. I chose the latter.

Embracing change doesn't mean ignoring fear. It means acknowledging it, feeling it, and stepping forward anyway. I began small—adapting to new routines, exploring new friendships, and accepting the new reality. Each adjustment, no matter how minor, taught me resilience, patience, and adaptability. I realized that life's beauty often hides in the unknown, waiting for us to take the leap.

One of the most profound lessons about change is that it reveals character.

When circumstances shift, comfort disappears, and expectations are challenged, who we truly are becomes visible. I remember struggling with a sudden change in my academic schedule.

Classes were rescheduled, responsibilities increased, and my familiar rhythm disrupted. Initially, I was frustrated, stressed, and tempted to give up. But by facing the challenge, adapting, and reorganizing, I discovered my own resourcefulness, patience, and determination. Change had shown me strengths I didn't know I possessed.

Change also teaches flexibility. Life rarely unfolds exactly as we plan. I once prepared extensively for a school performance, rehearsing every line, gesture, and expression. But on the day of the event, a sudden technical issue forced improvisation. Panic struck initially, but I adapted. I modified my delivery, trusted my instincts, and embraced the unexpected. The performance wasn't perfect, but it was authentic, memorable, and empowering. Change had pushed me to innovate, improvise, and trust myself.

I've learned that change is a teacher of humility. It reminds us that control is limited, certainty is rare, and life is unpredictable. Accepting this truth shifts perspective. Instead of resisting, complaining, or blaming, we can choose to learn, adapt, and grow. Every change, whether desired or imposed, is an opportunity for reflection, discovery, and evolution.

Embracing change also fosters courage. It requires stepping into the unknown, leaving familiarity behind, and facing uncertainty with confidence. I recall joining a new club at school—something completely unfamiliar, where I didn't know anyone. Fear whispered that I would fail, be judged, or feel out of place. But I reminded myself of past experiences: small wins, failures, self-love, listening, and inner reflection had prepared me for challenges. I stepped forward, engaged openly, and discovered new friendships, skills, and experiences. Courage, I realized, grows when we embrace change intentionally.

Change strengthens resilience. Life's unexpected turns—family moves, friendships shifting, academic pressures—test patience, adaptability, and perspective. I remember dealing with a sudden illness in the family that disrupted my daily life. Initially, stress, fear, and helplessness overwhelmed me. But by accepting the reality, adjusting routines, and finding ways to cope, I developed emotional resilience, empathy, and maturity. Each challenge reminded me that resilience is born from adapting to change, not resisting it.

Another aspect of embracing change is letting go. Sometimes, growth demands releasing habits, relationships, or mindsets that no longer serve us. I learned to recognize patterns that limited creativity, confidence, or happiness. Letting go was uncomfortable, but necessary. It allowed space for new experiences, learning, and personal evolution. Change often comes disguised as loss, but loss can create opportunity.

I've also realized that embracing change nurtures curiosity. When I face new environments, perspectives, or challenges, I begin to ask questions, explore possibilities, and observe with attentiveness. Change encourages learning, innovation, and awareness. I remember exploring a new city for a school trip—initially nervous, unsure, and overwhelmed. But stepping out, observing, and engaging led to discovery, adventure, and personal growth. The experience taught me that curiosity thrives when fear of change diminishes.

Change also enhances self-awareness. It exposes strengths, weaknesses, fears, and desires. I recall adapting to online learning during sudden school closures. At first, I struggled with focus, motivation, and discipline. But over time, I learned to structure my environment, manage time, and cultivate independence. The experience revealed resilience and adaptability I hadn't acknowledged before. Change, in its challenge, reflected my own growth back to me.

The moral of embracing change is intertwined with perspective. Life will constantly evolve—people leave, opportunities shift, circumstances fluctuate. Viewing change as a threat limits growth; viewing it as a teacher fosters resilience, creativity, and empowerment. I remind myself daily: comfort may feel safe, but growth lives in the unknown.

I also learned that embracing change deepens relationships. Accepting others' transformations—in thought, behavior, or circumstance—allows bonds to evolve instead of breaking. I remember a friend who changed interests drastically. Initially, I felt left behind, disconnected, and unsure how to relate. But by accepting their change, observing, and engaging openly, our friendship adapted, matured, and strengthened. Change, when embraced, preserves connections while fostering individuality.

Embracing change requires self-compassion. It is easy to feel inadequate when circumstances shift, or progress stalls. But reflecting inwardly and acknowledging effort, courage, and growth nurtures confidence and patience. I learned to say: "It's okay to feel uncertain, to struggle, to adapt slowly. Growth is happening, even if it isn't obvious."

Finally, embracing change reminds me that life is a journey, not a destination. Each change, challenge, or shift is a stepping stone, a teacher, and an opportunity for reflection. I now approach life with openness, curiosity, and courage. I trust that even when the path twists unexpectedly, I possess the strength, creativity, and resilience to navigate it.

So, I welcome change—in myself, in others, and in the world around me. I embrace uncertainty, adapt to challenges, explore new possibilities, and celebrate growth. Change, I have realized, is not an obstacle but a companion, guiding me toward deeper understanding, strength, and authenticity.

The moral is clear: embracing change is essential for growth, resilience, and self-discovery. Life will constantly evolve, but by facing change with courage, openness, and curiosity, we transform fear into opportunity, uncertainty into learning, and disruption into empowerment. Change, when embraced, becomes a teacher, a guide, and a doorway to becoming our best selves.

Chapter 22

Finding Your Voice

"Your voice is your signature; let no one dictate its tone."

For a long time, I spoke only when necessary. I observed, nodded, and adapted to others' expectations, afraid that my thoughts, opinions, or ideas might be wrong, insignificant, or unwelcome. I thought blending in was safer than standing out, silence wiser than speaking up. But life, in its persistent way, taught me a truth I could not ignore: finding your voice is one of the most powerful acts of self-respect, courage, and authenticity.

I remember my earliest experience of speaking up. It was a classroom discussion, and a topic came up about a book that everyone seemed to interpret the same way. I disagreed. My heart raced. I hesitated. I feared judgment, laughter, or dismissal. But something inside me nudged me to speak. I raised my hand and shared my perspective, carefully but confidently. The room went quiet, and I waited. Then, to my surprise, some classmates nodded in agreement, and the teacher smiled. That moment taught me: my thoughts matter, and my voice deserves to be heard. Finding your voice is more than speaking loudly or frequently; it is about expressing truth, clarity, and authenticity. It is about communicating ideas, feelings, and beliefs with honesty, even if it feels uncomfortable. I learned that the journey to find one's voice begins with self-awareness—understanding your values, your passions, your emotions, and your boundaries.

I began practicing by writing, journaling, and reflecting. I explored my thoughts deeply, questioning why I felt certain emotions or believed particular ideas. By listening to myself first, I learned to articulate my thoughts with clarity. I realized that before others can hear your voice, you must first hear yourself.

There were moments of doubt. Fear of judgment, rejection, or failure often whispered louder than my determination. I remember participating in a school debate where my arguments were challenged fiercely. Initially, I faltered, hesitated, and second-guessed myself. But I reminded myself: confidence is built in the act of speaking, not in perfection. I collected my thoughts, expressed them clearly, and engaged respectfully. The debate wasn't flawless, but it was authentic, and it strengthened my voice.

Finding your voice also requires courage to confront opposition. Not everyone will agree, accept, or appreciate your perspective. I once shared my opinion in a group project about a new approach, and several members resisted, insisting their way was better. I felt nervous, even intimidated. But by calmly explaining my reasoning, listening to feedback, and standing by my ideas without arrogance, I found balance—asserting my voice while remaining respectful.

Courage is not aggression; it is confidence and clarity in expressing truth. Another lesson I discovered is that voice is shaped by action. Words alone are insufficient; your actions must align with your beliefs. I remember advocating for a school initiative to reduce plastic waste. I spoke passionately, but also modeled the behavior—using reusable bottles, organizing awareness campaigns, and inspiring peers through example. Action amplified my voice, and authenticity resonated louder than mere words.

Finding your voice is deeply personal. It is shaped by experiences, values, and growth. I noticed that when I suppressed emotions, avoided speaking, or conformed to expectations, I felt fragmented and powerless. But when I expressed myself honestly, whether through writing, art, conversation, or advocacy, I felt empowered, connected, and authentic. Your voice reflects who you are, and embracing it fosters self-respect and confidence.

I have also learned that listening complements speaking. A strong voice does not dominate; it engages, reflects, and understands. By actively listening to others, I discovered nuance, perspective, and empathy, which strengthened how I expressed my own ideas. Communication is a dialogue, not a monologue, and finding your voice means participating with awareness, respect, and authenticity.

Vulnerability is another key aspect of finding your voice. Sharing feelings, fears, or struggles requires courage because it exposes parts of yourself that may be judged or misunderstood. I remember confiding in a friend about my anxieties regarding a competition. Speaking openly was terrifying, yet it brought relief, understanding, and connection. Vulnerability amplifies authenticity, and authenticity strengthens voice.

The journey to finding your voice also teaches perseverance. Some words may fall on deaf ears, ideas may be dismissed, or perspectives may be misunderstood. I recall presenting an original poem in school, only to face criticism and indifference from some peers. Initially, I felt disheartened, questioning whether my voice mattered. But I continued writing, refining, and expressing. Over time, my voice gained clarity, confidence, and resonance. Persistence ensures that your voice evolves, strengthens, and reaches those who are ready to hear it.

I've realized that finding your voice empowers others. When we express our truth authentically, we inspire, validate, and encourage those around us. I have seen classmates gain courage after witnessing me speak honestly, friends opening up after I shared my experiences, and younger students seeking guidance when I advocated for causes I believed in. A voice, when nurtured, becomes a tool for connection, change, and empowerment.

Self-love underpins finding your voice. I cannot speak confidently, assert boundaries, or express needs without valuing myself. I learned that respecting my thoughts, feelings, and experiences allowed me to communicate authentically. Self-doubt often silences the voice, but self-respect amplifies it. Your voice is strongest when rooted in your worth.

I also discovered that humor, creativity, and subtlety are part of voice. Not every message needs to be loud or serious; tone, style, and delivery matter. I experimented with storytelling, metaphors, and humor to express perspectives in ways that felt genuine and impactful. Your voice reflects not only what you say but how you say it.

Finding your voice is liberating. I now approach conversations, debates, creative work, and personal expression with confidence, clarity, and courage. I understand that my voice may evolve, shift, or adapt, but its essence remains rooted in authenticity, reflection, and integrity. Silence may sometimes be necessary, but it is never a substitute for truth.

I encourage myself and others to take risks, speak truth, and embrace authenticity. Share ideas, express feelings, advocate for values, and stand for what you believe in—even when it feels uncomfortable. Each word, each act of expression, strengthens identity, confidence, and connection.

The moral is clear: finding your voice is an act of courage, authenticity, and empowerment. Speak your truth, express your thoughts, honor your emotions, and let your voice resonate—not to dominate, but to connect, inspire, and live authentically. Silence may seem safe, but your voice carries the power to shape life, influence others, and reflect your truest self.

Chapter 23

The Strength in Forgiveness

"We are not meant to be polished stones; we are meant to be mountains, wild and scarred by the storms we've survived."

Forgiveness has always seemed paradoxical to me. How could letting go of hurt, anger, or betrayal possibly make someone stronger? For years, I carried grudges, replayed wrongs, and allowed resentment to shape my thoughts. I thought forgiveness meant weakness or surrender. But life, in its subtle and relentless way, taught me that true strength lies in the act of forgiving—not for others, but for oneself.

I remember the first time I confronted the power of forgiveness. A close friend had betrayed my trust. I was hurt, angry, and confused. I wanted to lash out, to prove them wrong, to ensure they felt the same pain I did. But every time I replayed the event, I felt more exhausted, bitter, and trapped. The pain I carried was mine, not theirs. That's when it struck me: holding onto anger only chained me, while forgiveness could set me free.

Forgiveness is not forgetting. It is not pretending that the hurt never happened or excusing the behavior. It is a conscious decision to release the weight of resentment, to reclaim peace, and to redirect energy toward growth. I began practicing forgiveness first in small ways—letting go of minor arguments, overlooking mistakes, and reframing misunderstandings. Each time, I felt lighter, clearer, and more resilient.

I learned that forgiveness is a reflection of

self-respect. By forgiving, I was not validating wrong actions; I was valuing my own peace, growth, and emotional freedom. I realized that resentment, anger, and grudges are forms of self-imprisonment. Choosing forgiveness became an act of courage—the courage to prioritize inner well-being over pride, ego, or revenge.

One of the most powerful lessons came when I forgave someone who had hurt me deeply. Initially, the process was painful and confusing. My mind wavered between resentment and relief. But I journaled my thoughts, reflected on the circumstances, and asked: "What lesson can I take from this? How can I release pain without losing strength?" The answer was simple yet profound: forgiveness was not about them, it was about reclaiming myself.

I discovered that forgiveness nurtures emotional intelligence. It teaches empathy, perspective, and understanding. I began trying to see situations from others' viewpoints, acknowledging their flaws, limitations, or struggles. This did not justify wrongdoing, but it humanized people and eased the intensity of my anger. Forgiveness transformed not just relationships, but my own emotional resilience and maturity.

Forgiveness also requires humility. Admitting that I could have responded differently, recognizing my own mistakes, and accepting imperfection allowed me to forgive more genuinely. I learned that life is messy, people are flawed, and holding onto rigid expectations leads only to suffering. Humility opened space for compassion, understanding, and authentic healing.

I remember a situation at school when a teammate sabotaged a group project. My initial reaction was fury, embarrassment, and desire for retaliation. But through reflection, I realized that holding anger would only hinder my focus, creativity, and progress. By forgiving, I regained control over my emotions, prioritized the work, and even managed to repair the relationship.

Strength, I realized, was the ability to act wisely even in the face of hurt.

Forgiveness does not always involve reconciliation. Sometimes, it means releasing emotional attachment while maintaining boundaries. I learned to forgive toxic behavior without subjecting myself to repeated harm. Forgiveness became an internal process, independent of the other person's acknowledgment or apology. This realization was liberating: I could find peace without needing validation from others.

The moral lesson deepened when I reflected on my own mistakes. I recognized moments when I had hurt others, intentionally or unintentionally. Forgiving myself was equally vital.

Self-forgiveness is often harder than forgiving others because it forces confrontation with guilt, shame, and regret. I learned that acknowledging flaws, accepting responsibility, and moving forward is an essential part of growth.

Forgiveness also strengthens relationships. By releasing resentment, I was able to rebuild trust, communicate openly, and cultivate understanding. I observed that relationships grow not when conflict is absent, but when hurt is addressed, processed, and released. Forgiveness fosters connection, empathy, and emotional depth.

I realized that forgiveness encourages emotional liberation. Anger, bitterness, and grudges consume energy, cloud judgment, and limit potential. By choosing to forgive, I unlocked mental clarity, focus, and the ability to invest in meaningful experiences. Life felt lighter, relationships richer, and opportunities more visible.

Forgiveness is a process, not an instant act. Some wounds take time to heal, some betrayals linger, and some pain resurfaces unexpectedly. I learned patience, reflection, and compassion in navigating these moments. Journaling, meditation, and honest conversations became tools to process emotions and reinforce the commitment to forgive.

I also discovered that forgiveness fuels resilience. Life will inevitably bring disappointment, betrayal, or hurt. By practicing forgiveness, I developed the ability to recover faster, think clearly, and respond with strength rather than reactivity. Forgiveness is not weakness; it is a strategic choice that preserves power, energy, and clarity.

A particularly profound lesson came when I forgave a parent for a misunderstanding during my teenage years. The incident had caused months of tension and sadness. Forgiving them did not erase the event, but it restored peace, love, and understanding. I realized that forgiveness heals not only the present pain but also generations of miscommunication, resentment, and emotional baggage.

I began to see forgiveness as a form of courage intertwined with wisdom. It requires facing uncomfortable emotions, relinquishing control over outcomes, and trusting that peace and growth are more valuable than revenge or pride. Courage without forgiveness often leads to bitterness; forgiveness without courage is shallow. Together, they create emotional empowerment.

I practiced expressing forgiveness verbally, in writing, and silently. Each method offered a different dimension: speaking it aloud reinforced resolve, writing clarified thoughts, and silent reflection cultivated internal peace. The act of forgiveness, I realized, was less about ceremony and more about intent, awareness, and emotional commitment.

I also observed that forgiving others often led to unexpected compassion. I felt lighter, more patient, and more understanding in situations unrelated to the original hurt. Forgiveness became a lens through which I approached life—a filter that softened conflicts, clarified intentions, and enhanced empathy.

Forgiveness strengthened my inner voice. By releasing resentment, I reclaimed mental space, clarity, and energy. I became more decisive, confident, and present. Forgiveness was no longer an abstract moral; it became a practical tool for emotional empowerment, clarity, and resilience.

Finally, I realized that forgiveness is a lifelong practice. Some hurts are easily released, others resurface repeatedly. The commitment to forgive, reflect, and grow must be renewed continuously. Life will test patience, ego, and emotions, but each act of forgiveness builds strength, wisdom, and freedom.

The moral is clear: true strength is found in forgiveness. Forgiveness is not weakness, surrender, or forgetfulness; it is courage, liberation, and self-respect. By forgiving others and oneself, we reclaim peace, nurture growth, and cultivate resilience. Life may bring hurt, betrayal, or mistakes, but forgiveness transforms pain into empowerment, anger into clarity, and wounds into wisdom.

Chapter 24

The Art of Patience

"To be 'not for everyone' is the greatest freedom, for it means you are finally and entirely for yourself."

Patience has always felt like a quiet, almost invisible strength. When I was younger, I believed that speed, efficiency, and immediate results defined success. Waiting felt uncomfortable, frustrating, even pointless. But life has a way of teaching lessons in its own time, and I realized that patience is not about waiting idly—it's about learning, observing, and growing while time unfolds.

I remember a moment in middle school when I was struggling with a personal project. I had invested days of effort, yet results were slow, and progress seemed almost invisible. I grew restless, questioning why others seemed to achieve so quickly. My frustration mounted, and I wanted to give up. But a teacher, noticing my impatience, said something simple yet profound: "Patience isn't about waiting; it's about what you do while you wait." That sentence lingered with me, like a quiet whisper of truth. From that day, I began experimenting with patience—not as passive waiting, but as active engagement with the present. I learned to focus on small improvements, to appreciate tiny achievements, and to accept that meaningful growth rarely happens overnight. Patience became a lens through which I could observe life with clarity rather than rush through it in anxiety.

Patience also taught me humility. I had to acknowledge that I cannot control every outcome or dictate the pace of life. I remember practicing for a school recital, rehearsing tirelessly yet repeatedly missing perfection. At first, frustration consumed me, but gradually, I learned to accept mistakes as part of learning. Patience allowed me to embrace imperfection, understand limitations, and persist with grace. Waiting, I realized, was not weakness—it was wisdom.

One of the most challenging aspects of patience is resisting the urge for instant gratification. In today's world, everything feels immediate—messages, achievements, recognition. I noticed that whenever I rushed, I often overlooked details, lost depth, or made errors. Practicing patience taught me that slow progress often produces the strongest results, and that resilience grows when we honor natural timing.

I also discovered that patience enhances empathy. When I allow myself to pause and observe, I can understand others better—their struggles, fears, and limitations. I remember a classmate who often frustrated me with repeated mistakes. Initially, I reacted with annoyance and judgment. But by taking a step back, observing patiently, and reflecting on their perspective, I realized that they were learning at their own pace. Patience allowed me to respond with kindness instead of irritation.

Patience strengthens self-awareness. I noticed my impulses, triggers, and anxieties, and learned to pause before reacting. I journaled my frustrations, reflected on my emotions, and considered alternative responses. Gradually, patience became an internal discipline, a way of controlling reactions, nurturing reflection, and fostering growth.

Another lesson I learned is that

patience is closely tied to trust—trust in yourself, in the process, and in life itself. There were moments when I doubted whether my efforts would ever payoff: a competition I had trained for months, a creative project that seemed stagnant, or a personal goal that faced repeated obstacles. Yet, by persevering with patience, I observed that results often emerge in their own time, sometimes unexpectedly and more beautifully than I had imagined.

Patience also nurtures resilience. Life tests us with delays, setbacks, and uncertainties. I remember preparing for an inter-school event that required coordination, planning, and collaboration. Unexpected issues arose—changes in schedule, missing resources, and miscommunication. Initially, I felt frustrated and overwhelmed. But I reminded myself to breathe, to take one step at a time, and to approach challenges with calm determination. The event ultimately succeeded, and the lessons I learned about adaptability, calmness, and perseverance were far more valuable than the event itself.

I realized that patience strengthens relationships too. People grow, learn, and evolve at their own pace. By practicing patience, I learned to give space to friends, family, and peers without judgment. I understood that conflicts often dissolve when we pause, listen, and allow time for understanding. Patience transforms tension into dialogue, frustration into empathy, and impatience into connection.

I also discovered that patience allows creativity to flourish. Many times, I rushed through writing assignments or personal projects, seeking quick completion. The results were shallow, uninspired, or incomplete. By slowing down, experimenting, and allowing ideas to develop naturally, my creativity expanded. Patience nurtured insight, imagination, and originality.

The moral of patience became particularly clear when I faced personal disappointment—a rejection from something I had deeply hoped for. Initially, sadness and anger overwhelmed me. I wanted immediate consolation, instant validation, and quick solutions. But by accepting the process, reflecting on lessons, and giving myself time to heal, I discovered clarity, strength, and a renewed perspective. Patience became not just a skill, but a life philosophy.

I noticed that patience often intersects with self-discipline. Waiting without direction is futile; patience coupled with purposeful effort leads to progress. I learned to set small, achievable goals, track incremental growth, and celebrate milestones while continuing toward the larger aim. This approach transformed impatience into structured persistence.

Patience also cultivates gratitude. By slowing down and observing life carefully, I began appreciating subtle joys—a friend's laughter, the warmth of sunlight, the satisfaction of small accomplishments. Patience allows us to notice life's nuances instead of constantly rushing toward the next thing.

Another aspect is emotional regulation. When I practice patience, my reactions become measured, thoughtful, and constructive. I no longer respond impulsively to frustration, criticism, or setbacks. Instead, I pause, reflect, and choose my response. This has strengthened my confidence, emotional resilience, and interpersonal skills.

I've realized that patience is a bridge between intention and outcome. It transforms waiting into a period of growth, reflection, and preparation. I remember applying this during an academic challenge that initially seemed insurmountable. By patiently studying, revising, and seeking guidance, I eventually succeeded far beyond what I had expected. The journey itself, guided by patience, was as valuable as the result.

Patience requires self-compassion. We often criticize ourselves for perceived delays, mistakes, or slow progress. I learned to treat myself gently, acknowledging effort, valuing persistence, and celebrating gradual growth. Compassion and patience together create a fertile ground for self-improvement.

Finally, I discovered that patience brings peace. In a world obsessed with speed, deadlines, and immediate results, patience allows us to breathe, reflect, and engage deeply with life. It reminds us that growth, understanding, and achievement take time, and that rushing often diminishes quality and insight.

The moral is clear: patience is not passive waiting; it is active, conscious growth, reflection, and resilience. Life unfolds in its own time, and by embracing patience, we cultivate strength, empathy, clarity, creativity, and peace. Impatience may offer temporary relief, but patience builds enduring character and lasting fulfillment.

Chapter 25

The Balance of Ambition

"The most beautiful love story you will ever read is the one where you forgive and embrace the person you used to be."

Ambition has always fascinated me. From a young age, I admired those who dreamed big, worked hard, and achieved remarkable goals. I too carried dreams that seemed enormous—ideas, projects, and aspirations that fueled my days and nights. Yet, as I grew older, I realized that ambition, when unchecked, can be both a driving force and a silent burden. The key, I discovered, lies in finding the balance between desire and mindfulness, drive and peace.

I remember my first encounter with this lesson. I had set a goal to excel in a school competition
— not just participate, but dominate. I spent countless hours preparing, strategizing, and pushing myself beyond comfort. At first, the energy was exhilarating, the focus empowering. But soon, the excitement blurred into obsession. I neglected friendships, skipped meals, and lost sight of simple joys. I realized that ambition without balance was draining rather than fulfilling.

Balance in ambition does not mean abandoning goals. Rather, it is about aligning efforts with well-being, values, and clarity of purpose. I began reflecting: Why am I pursuing this goal? Is it for recognition, self-growth, or simply comparison with others? This reflection helped me redirect energy toward meaningful, intentional action rather than reactive, pressured achievement.

I noticed that balanced ambition requires patience, which I had learned in the previous chapter. Ambitious pursuits often take time, effort, and incremental progress. Impatience, unrealistic expectations, and constant comparison can sabotage the journey. By practicing patience, I began to appreciate small milestones, celebrate incremental growth, and trust the process rather than obsess over immediate results.

Another lesson I discovered is that ambition should not compromise integrity or empathy. I observed peers who achieved success by undermining others, manipulating situations, or cutting corners. Their achievements were hollow, and their relationships suffered. I decided early on that my ambition would never override my values or harm others, even if it meant slower progress or greater effort. Balance is about success without sacrificing character.

Ambition also interacts with self-awareness. I learned to recognize my strengths, weaknesses, and limitations. By understanding where I excelled and where I needed growth, I could pursue goals realistically while stretching my potential. Overextending without awareness often leads to burnout, disappointment, or frustration. Balanced ambition blends confidence with humility, effort with reflection, and action with wisdom.

I remember a creative project where my ideas were ambitious—far beyond what seemed achievable. Initially, I felt anxious about whether I could meet expectations. But instead of abandoning the project, I broke it into smaller steps, sought guidance, and maintained consistent effort. The outcome was remarkable—not because I rushed, but because I balanced vision with strategy, energy with planning, and aspiration with reality.

Balanced ambition also requires boundaries. I realized that working relentlessly without rest or reflection diminishes effectiveness and joy. I incorporated routines for rest, hobbies, and social connection, ensuring that ambition fueled life rather than consumed it. Boundaries became tools to sustain long-term growth and preserve mental, emotional, and physical well-being.

I observed that ambition, when balanced, inspires others. Friends and peers often approached me for guidance, motivation, or collaboration. They admired not just the results I achieved, but the mindful, ethical, and resilient approach I maintained. Ambition, balanced with integrity and awareness, becomes a model—not just for personal success, but for positive influence.

Another important aspect is reflection. Ambition can drive us forward, but without reflection, we risk losing direction or pursuing goals that no longer align with values. I started journaling regularly, assessing my progress, motivations, and satisfaction. Reflection allowed me to adjust paths, embrace new opportunities, and ensure that my ambition remained purposeful rather than compulsive.

I also discovered that balance in ambition fosters gratitude. While striving for future goals, it is easy to overlook current achievements, learning experiences, and supportive people. I learned to pause, acknowledge progress, and appreciate those who supported me. Gratitude prevents ambition from becoming a source of dissatisfaction or endless longing.

Failure, I realized, is an inevitable part of ambition. Ambitious goals often involve risk, uncertainty, and setbacks. Early in my journey, I experienced disappointment when a project I invested in deeply failed. At first, I felt devastated, questioning my abilities and purpose. But by embracing reflection, patience, and perseverance, I realized that failure is not the opposite of success; it is a vital part of growth, learning, and refinement of ambition.

Balanced ambition also includes adaptability. Life rarely unfolds exactly as planned. Goals may shift, circumstances may change, and priorities may evolve. By remaining flexible while staying true to core values, I learned to pursue ambition with both determination and openness. This balance reduces frustration and maximizes opportunity.

I discovered that true ambition is deeply personal. It should not be dictated by competition, social pressure, or comparison. I remember observing classmates chasing awards purely for recognition or status. Their external success felt hollow. I resolved that my ambition would focus on personal growth, meaningful impact, and authentic achievement, not external validation.

Ambition, when balanced, also strengthens relationships. I learned to involve others in collaborative projects, to listen, respect, and inspire. Success becomes more fulfilling when shared, and relationships remain intact rather than strained. Ambition without balance can isolate, but balanced ambition enriches community, support, and connection.

Another insight was the interplay between ambition and self-compassion. I recognized moments when I pushed too hard, felt frustrated, or doubted progress. By treating myself kindly, accepting mistakes, and valuing effort over immediate perfection, I maintained motivation without unnecessary self-criticism. Self-compassion fuels sustainable ambition.

Balanced ambition creates a sense of purpose and direction. Goals provide motivation, structure, and meaning, but balance ensures that pursuit does not become obsession. I learned to set priorities, adjust expectations, and cultivate resilience, ensuring that ambition strengthens life rather than diminishes it.

I also observed the subtle beauty of ambition aligned with curiosity. When goals are fueled by genuine interest and passion, rather than fear or comparison, work becomes joy, learning becomes exploration, and achievement becomes meaningful. Ambition becomes not a burden, but a fulfilling journey of growth and discovery.

Finally, I realized that balance in ambition is lifelong. Goals, desires, and circumstances evolve, requiring continuous reflection, adjustment, and integration of values, effort, and self-care.

Balanced ambition is a dance—a rhythm between striving and accepting, effort and patience, desire and reflection.

The moral is clear: ambition is powerful, but only when balanced with mindfulness, integrity, patience, and self-awareness. Strive boldly, pursue passionately, and dream expansively, but never sacrifice values, peace, or well-being. Ambition fuels growth, but balance ensures that growth is meaningful, sustainable, and empowering.

Chapter 26

The Courage to Let Go

"Releasing what weighs you down is the first step to soaring."

Letting go has always felt like a paradox to me. How could releasing something I held dear—a person, a dream, or even a belief—ever feel like strength rather than defeat? For years, I clung tightly, afraid of emptiness, fear, or change. But life, in its quiet persistence, taught me that true courage is not in holding on, but in knowing when to let go.

I remember the first time I truly experienced this lesson. A friendship I had treasured for years began to drift apart. Small misunderstandings grew into tension, and slowly, distance formed where connection once thrived. I felt a deep ache—a desire to repair, to reclaim, to force continuity. Yet, no matter how hard I tried, the bond could not return to its original state. I realized then that some things are meant to evolve or end, not because we failed, but because life is fluid. Holding on too tightly only prevents growth.

Letting go does not mean giving up or being weak. It means recognizing reality, accepting impermanence, and making space for new experiences. I began to apply this understanding to other areas of life—grudges, past mistakes, unfulfilled dreams. I realized that clinging to the past often hinders progress, clouds judgment, and drains energy. Courage, I learned, is choosing to release what no longer serves you while honoring its place in your journey.

I recall a time when I struggled with letting go of a goal I had deeply desired—an opportunity I had imagined for months. The rejection was crushing, and I resisted the idea of moving on. But as days passed, I reflected and realized that clinging to disappointment was keeping me trapped. By accepting reality and letting go, I freed myself to explore new paths and unexpected opportunities. Courage, I realized, involves trusting the flow of life while releasing attachment to outcomes.

Letting go requires honesty—with oneself and with others. I had to confront uncomfortable truths: that some relationships were toxic, some dreams unrealistic, and some patterns self-destructive. Denial or avoidance only prolongs suffering. By embracing truth, I could release without resentment, bitterness,

or regret. Courageous letting go is rooted in clarity, awareness, and emotional maturity.
One of the most profound lessons came when I forgave and let go of a long-held resentment. For months, I had replayed an incident in my mind, nurturing anger and pain. At first, I thought forgiveness would be enough. But true peace arrived only when I let go entirely—not just of resentment, but of the story I had built around it. I felt lighter, freer, and more capable of embracing life fully.
Letting go also teaches resilience. Life is unpredictable, and setbacks are inevitable. I noticed that those who resisted change often struggled longer, while those who released attachment adapted, learned, and grew. Courage is about flexibility, adaptability, and the willingness to embrace the unknown.

I discovered that letting go nurtures emotional intelligence. When I release control, expectations, or anger, I become more aware of my feelings, triggers, and desires. I respond thoughtfully rather than react impulsively. I observed that emotional clarity arises not from clinging, but from surrendering what cannot be controlled.

Letting go is a form of self-respect. By releasing harmful relationships, unproductive habits, or unattainable goals, I honor my own well-being, peace, and growth. I realized that self-respect sometimes requires saying "no" to the familiar, the comfortable, or the expected. Courage is rooted in valuing oneself more than clinging to what harms or limits one's growth.

Another lesson I learned is that letting go encourages forgiveness—of others and of oneself. Holding onto mistakes, regrets, or grudges creates chains that limit freedom. I practiced writing letters I never sent, meditating on past hurts, and consciously choosing to release them. Each act of letting go strengthened inner peace, clarity, and confidence.

Letting go also fosters growth and creativity. When I freed myself from old patterns or outdated beliefs, new ideas, opportunities, and perspectives emerged. I realized that clinging often blocks evolution, while courageously releasing opens space for transformation. Life felt more expansive, exciting, and full of possibility.

I recall a particularly difficult moment when I had to let go of someone I loved deeply. Part of me wanted to resist, to negotiate, to hold on. But love, I learned, does not always mean possession. True love sometimes requires letting go, respecting freedom, and trusting that life will bring what is meant to be. Letting go did not diminish love; it transformed it into acceptance, compassion, and peace.

I discovered that letting go requires practice. Some releases are immediate, others gradual. Some days feel lighter, others heavy with nostalgia or fear. Journaling, reflection, and mindfulness became tools to navigate this process. Courage is not the absence of fear, but the choice to act in spite of it.

Another insight was the relationship between letting go and gratitude. By releasing attachment, I learned to appreciate what remained—the lessons, memories, and growth from experiences past. Gratitude transforms release from loss into acknowledgment of value and meaning.

Letting go also enhances decision-making. When I am not weighed down by attachment or fear, I can make clearer, wiser choices. I observed that many poor decisions arise from clinging to comfort, pride, or expectations—rather than seeing reality with honesty and courage.

I realized that letting go strengthens relationships. Sometimes, stepping back, releasing control, or accepting impermanence can actually improve connection rather than damaging it. By allowing others to grow, evolve, or make different choices, I honor both their journey and my own. Courage in relationships is recognizing that control is an illusion, and freedom fosters trust, respect, and depth.

Another aspect is patience intertwined with letting go. Release does not always produce instant peace or understanding. Some wounds take time to heal, some patterns recur, and some endings feel abrupt. Patience allows letting go to settle gradually, nurturing acceptance, wisdom, and serenity.

Self-compassion is also essential. Letting go can feel like failure, rejection, or loss. By treating oneself kindly, acknowledging effort, and embracing imperfection, courage is strengthened rather than diminished. Release becomes empowerment rather than despair.

Finally, I discovered that letting go is a continuous practice. Life will present new challenges, losses, and transitions. Courage is renewing the choice to release, adapt, and trust repeatedly, even when the heart hesitates. Each act of letting go builds emotional strength, clarity, and resilience. The moral is clear: courage is found in letting go. Release does not signify weakness or surrender; it is a deliberate, brave choice to embrace growth, peace, and freedom. Life flows, relationships evolve, and dreams change. By letting go, we honor ourselves, respect others, and make space for transformation, joy, and authenticity.

Chapter 27

The Power of Self-Belief

"Authenticity is not a destination; it's the continuous, quiet refusal to edit your own life for someone else's comfort."

Self-belief is a strange thing. For the longest time, I thought confidence was something you either had or didn't. I watched others seem fearless, bold, and sure of themselves, while I doubted every word, every action, and even every thought.

But life has a way of teaching that self-belief is not about arrogance or perfection—it is about trust in one's own abilities, choices, and voice, even in the face of fear or uncertainty.

I remember the first time I realized the real power of self-belief. I had been selected to give a speech in front of the entire school—something I had never done before. My heart raced, my palms were sweaty, and every step toward the stage felt heavy with doubt. I thought, what if I forget my words? What if they laugh at me? But then, I reminded myself of every hour I had practiced, every idea I had carefully crafted, every bit of courage I had quietly gathered. That small inner voice whispered: "You are capable. You are prepared. Believe in yourself."

Stepping onto the stage, I didn't feel invincible, but I felt grounded. With each sentence, my confidence grew, not because I had conquered fear, but because I had chosen to trust myself despite it. That day, I discovered that self-belief is a quiet strength that grows from persistence, preparation, and inner conviction, not from approval or recognition.

Self-belief requires knowing your worth and embracing your unique qualities. In a world that constantly compares, criticizes, and pressures, it is easy to doubt oneself. I learned to silence the noise, focus on my own journey, and celebrate what made me unique. Every talent, passion, and perspective I had was a building block for confidence. Believing in oneself is not about being flawless; it's about being honest with your abilities and being willing to grow.

I remember struggling with a challenging assignment in science class. The concepts were complicated, the instructions unclear, and my first attempts failed. Frustration tempted me to give up, but I reminded myself that failure was not a reflection of inability. By patiently reviewing my notes, experimenting, and trusting my understanding, I eventually succeeded. That success wasn't just about solving the problem; it was a lesson that self-belief fuels perseverance, clarity, and resilience.

Another essential part of self-belief is trusting intuition. Often, I found myself questioning decisions, wondering if my choices were correct, or fearing the judgment of others. But experience taught me that my instincts are a reflection of my knowledge, values, and perspective. Listening to that inner voice, even when uncertain, became a source of courage and clarity. Self-belief is about aligning action with inner wisdom, rather than just external validation.

I observed that self-belief grows through small victories as much as big achievements. Completing a project, speaking up in class, or mastering a skill all helped to strengthen my confidence incrementally. Each success reinforced the truth that I was capable of more than I realized.

Conversely, setbacks became lessons rather than judgments, teaching me resilience, patience, and strategy.

I remember participating in a group project where everyone doubted my suggestions. I hesitated at first, feeling my ideas were too risky or unconventional. But I reminded myself that innovation often comes from the courage to believe in oneself. Speaking up, explaining my vision, and advocating for my ideas not only contributed meaningfully to the project but also earned respect. I realized that self-belief empowers expression, creativity, and influence.

Self-belief also involves embracing imperfection. I had to learn that confidence doesn't mean never failing or never making mistakes. True belief in oneself stems from understanding one's limitations, acknowledging errors, and persisting in one's efforts. Each mistake is not proof of incapability, but evidence of learning and growth. I practiced forgiving myself for missteps, focusing instead on what I could improve and achieve next.

I discovered that self-belief strengthens emotional resilience. Life often presents criticism, rejection, or doubt from others. Without confidence, these moments can shatter motivation and hope. But with self-belief, criticism becomes insight, rejection becomes redirection, and doubt becomes fuel to persist. It allows me to navigate challenges without losing faith in my potential.

There were moments when I compared myself to peers who seemed naturally talented or effortlessly successful. Initially, envy and insecurity clouded my judgment. But gradually, I realized that comparing journeys is meaningless—everyone moves at their own pace, faces unique challenges, and possesses different strengths. Self-belief means valuing your own journey and trusting your pace.

I also noticed that belief in oneself nurtures courage. Speaking up when intimidated, pursuing dreams when unsure, or taking risks when scared all require a foundation of confidence.

Without self-belief, fear dominates decisions. With it, courage becomes a natural extension, and action aligns with intention rather than hesitation. Self-belief strengthens relationships, too. When I trusted myself, I could contribute genuinely, communicate clearly, and engage authentically. Others responded to that with confidence, respect, and integrity. I observed that self-assured individuals often attract collaboration, trust, and mutual support because their clarity inspires others.

Another essential insight is that self-belief is a lifelong practice. Confidence isn't permanent; it fluctuates with circumstances, experiences, and moods. I learned to cultivate self-belief daily through reflection, acknowledging progress, setting small goals, and affirming my abilities. It becomes a muscle that strengthens with consistent care and attention.

I also discovered that self-belief is closely tied to passion. Confidence grows when pursuing what genuinely matters to you—projects, causes, or skills that resonate deeply. Passion provides direction, motivation, and energy, while self-belief ensures persistence, courage, and resilience. Together, they create unstoppable momentum.

I recall facing a personal challenge: presenting a poem I had written to a large audience. Nervousness and fear of judgment pressed heavily on me. But I trusted the value of my words, the effort I had put into crafting them, and my ability to communicate with sincerity. Speaking confidently, I saw how belief in my own voice transformed fear into presence, doubt into impact.

Self-belief also encourages independence. By

trusting my decisions, I could take ownership of actions, solve problems autonomously, and accept responsibility for outcomes. I learned that while advice, guidance, and collaboration are valuable, the foundation of success rests on trusting one's own judgment.

Another aspect is adaptability. Belief in oneself does not mean rigid certainty; it means being confident enough to adjust plans, pivot strategies, and embrace change. I learned that flexible self-belief empowers growth while maintaining stability.

I also realized that self-belief fosters a positive mindset. When I trust myself, I approach challenges with optimism rather than fear. Mistakes become lessons, obstacles become opportunities, and setbacks become stepping stones. Confidence transforms perspective, shaping experiences into empowerment rather than discouragement.

Through experiences, reflection, and practice, I internalized that self-belief is not ego. It is not about feeling superior, dominating others, or ignoring advice. It is about valuing one's abilities, trusting one's decisions, and pursuing growth with courage, clarity, and integrity. True self-belief strikes a balance between confidence and humility, ambition and patience, and determination and reflection.

I also observed that self-belief inspires perseverance. Goals often require sustained effort, repeated attempts, and resilience in the face of discouragement. Confidence in oneself provides the inner fuel to continue, adapt, and overcome challenges that might otherwise seem insurmountable. Lastly, self-belief brings freedom. When I trust my abilities and choices, I am liberated from fear, doubt, and dependency on external validation. Life becomes a canvas for action, creativity, and exploration. By believing in myself, I discovered that the power to shape my journey lies within me, and no obstacle can diminish it unless I let it. Self-belief is a quiet, steady force—not loud or boastful, but persistent, guiding, and transformative. It strengthens courage, nurtures resilience, inspires action, and shapes growth. It allows one to navigate life fully, boldly, and authentically, trusting that even in uncertainty, strength and wisdom are within

Chapter 28

The Lessons of Silence

"Resilience is not about never breaking; it is about learning the exact shape of your pieces so you know how to put them back together—stronger, but always real."

Silence is often misunderstood. People think it is emptiness, weakness, or absence, but I have come to realize that silence is far more powerful than words. It is a space where reflection, understanding, and strength reside. Learning to embrace silence–in thought, in action, and in response–has been one of the most transformative lessons of my life.

I remember a moment in class when an argument broke out over a minor disagreement. Voices rose, tempers flared, and everyone wanted to prove a point. I felt a strong urge to respond, to defend myself or my perspective. But something inside me paused. I chose silence–not avoidance, but conscious stillness. I observed, listened, and reflected. Later, when I finally spoke, my words were calm, precise, and impactful. That day I learned that silence is not absence; it is a form of power, a way to choose responses carefully rather than react impulsively.

Silence also teaches patience. In a world dominated by noise, constant communication, and immediate reactions, learning to pause is revolutionary. I noticed that when I resisted the urge to speak immediately, I could understand situations more clearly. I could observe emotions, motives, and dynamics that were invisible in haste. Patience through silence allows clarity to surface, decisions to strengthen, and emotions to settle.

I remember sitting alone in the library one rainy afternoon, overwhelmed by worries about exams, friendships, and my future. Everything inside me wanted to rush, plan, and fix. But I stayed silent, letting thoughts arrive and pass without judgment. In that quiet, I found unexpected insights: solutions that had been invisible in my noise, courage to confront fears, and the realization that some answers emerge only when we stop forcing them.

Silence is also a tool for self-reflection. I started journaling quietly, not just to write, but to listen to my own thoughts. Many of us spend life seeking approval, feedback, or validation from others, forgetting to check in with our own feelings. Silence allows connection with our inner self, revealing desires, fears, and truths that words often obscure. I discovered strengths, acknowledged weaknesses, and began shaping choices aligned with my authentic self. Another lesson I learned is that silence can communicate more than words. A pause, a glance, or a calm presence often speaks louder than arguments, explanations, or defense. I remember consoling a friend who was hurt and frustrated. I didn't try to offer solutions immediately; I simply sat beside them, listening quietly. That silence conveyed empathy, understanding, and presence—stronger than anything I could have said.

Silence also nurtures emotional control. When I learned to pause before responding in anger or frustration, I noticed the difference it made. I could approach situations with clarity, empathy, and precision rather than reacting impulsively.

Over time, silence became a shield and a tool—protecting relationships, preserving peace, and fostering wisdom.

I discovered that silence enhances observation. When I am silent, I notice details others often miss—expressions, tone, gestures, and subtle patterns. These observations deepen understanding, strengthen intuition, and improve decision-making. Life, I realized, communicates constantly; only silence allows us to truly listen.

Silence is also essential for creativity. Many of my ideas, poems, and reflections emerged during moments of quiet. When I allowed my mind to wander without noise or distraction, thoughts formed connections, insights appeared, and my imagination expanded. Silence became a canvas for innovation, introspection, and inspiration.

I also observed that silence requires courage. It is tempting to fill every moment with chatter, opinions, or reactions to prove presence or competence. Choosing silence, especially when provoked or pressured, demands self-discipline, confidence, and trust in oneself. It is a demonstration of strength, not passivity.

Letting silence guide interactions has also taught me humility. I realized that I don't always need to voice every thought, argue every point, or assert every opinion. Some situations benefit from listening, observing, and reflecting. Silence allows space for others' voices, fosters respect, and encourages meaningful dialogue rather than endless noise.

I remember a moment during a group discussion where everyone tried to dominate the conversation. I remained silent, simply listening, noting patterns, and reflecting. When I finally spoke, my point was concise, thoughtful, and impactful—more effective than anything I could have said in the rush of competing voices. Silence had amplified my influence rather than diminished it.

Silence also strengthens resilience. Life often presents challenges, criticism, or conflict. Responding immediately or impulsively can escalate problems or create regret. I learned to pause, process, and respond thoughtfully. This practice built patience, clarity, and strength, allowing me to face difficulties with composure rather than chaos.

Another insight is that silence fosters gratitude. In quiet moments, I reflected on life, relationships, and experiences. I became aware of blessings often overlooked in busyness and noise—supportive friends, small joys, personal growth, and opportunities. Silence creates the space to acknowledge and appreciate what truly matters.

Silence is also a source of mindfulness. I practiced sitting quietly, observing my breath, and letting thoughts drift without judgment. These moments taught me to live in the present, to engage fully with experiences, and to respond intentionally rather than habitually. Silence cultivates awareness, presence, and calmness.

I discovered that silence can be transformative in relationships. Misunderstandings, arguments, and tension often arise from reactive speech or unnecessary words. Choosing silence allows time to understand perspectives, reflect on emotions, and respond wisely. It creates room for empathy, reconciliation, and deeper connection.

I also realized that silence teaches acceptance. Not every situation can be changed, and not every problem has an immediate solution. By embracing quietude, I could release unnecessary worry, control, and expectation. Acceptance through silence brought freedom from frustration, anxiety, and resistance.

Self-compassion thrives in silence. Pausing, reflecting, and observing one's own thoughts nurtures kindness toward oneself. I learned to forgive mistakes, acknowledge effort, and embrace growth without harsh judgment. Silence becomes a tool for inner care and emotional nourishment.

I observed that silence enhances leadership and influence. Leaders who speak only when necessary, who listen actively, and who respond thoughtfully command respect and attention. Words become more powerful when chosen deliberately, and silence amplifies their impact.

Another lesson is that silence nurtures intuition. In quiet moments, insights emerge that are often drowned in noise, distractions, or external pressure. I began trusting my instincts, making decisions with clarity, and feeling more confident in my choices. Silence reveals truth, guides action, and strengthens judgment.

I discovered that silence fosters courage in personal expression. By observing first, reflecting deeply, and speaking intentionally, I could articulate thoughts, emotions, and ideas more authentically. Silence does not suppress voice; it empowers it.

Ultimately, I came to realize that silence is a form of liberation. In stillness, I am free from comparison, judgment, and expectation. I can observe, reflect, and create without distraction. Silence allows space for growth, understanding, and transformation. It is a companion, a guide, and a teacher—subtle, patient, and profound.

Through experiences, reflection, and practice, I internalized that silence is not emptiness, but a foundation for strength, clarity, empathy, creativity, and self-awareness. It teaches patience, presence, and resilience, guiding life with quiet wisdom rather than hurried noise.

Chapter 29

The Power of Choices

"The journey doesn't end when you become real; it only begins when you finally realize you were real all along."

Choices are the invisible threads that weave the fabric of life. From the moment we wake up to the moment we sleep, we are making decisions—some small, some monumental—each shaping our journey in ways we often cannot immediately see.

For the longest time, I underestimated the power of choice, assuming that circumstances, luck, or other people dictated the path. But over time, I realized that the ability to choose consciously, courageously, and thoughtfully is one of the greatest strengths anyone can possess.

I remember the first time I truly felt the weight of a significant choice. It was during a school competition where I had to decide between participating in an event I loved, risking failure, or sticking with a safer, more familiar option. My mind raced with possibilities, fears, and "what ifs." At first, indecision paralyzed me. But then I paused and asked myself, "What do I want?" What aligns with my values and passion? In that moment, clarity emerged. I chose the path that resonated with my heart, even if it carried uncertainty. That choice, regardless of outcome, became a profound act of self-trust.

Choices are not always about

extremes; often, they exist in subtle, everyday decisions. Choosing kindness over irritation, honesty over convenience, or effort over laziness may seem minor, but these choices accumulate, shaping character, relationships, and self-respect. I began to notice how my small decisions—helping a friend, speaking up in class, dedicating time to study—gradually formed a pattern of integrity and intentional living. Every choice is an investment in the person you are becoming.

One of the most challenging aspects of making a choice is accepting responsibility for the consequences. I recall a project where I took a calculated risk by approaching a topic in a way that differed from the initial suggestion. Initially, anxiety and doubt gnawed at me. Would it fail? Would I be judged? Yet, embracing responsibility, I committed fully. The result was a mix of success and lessons learned, but the most valuable outcome was the confidence that comes from owning decisions, both good and imperfect. Choice carries freedom, but freedom demands accountability.

I've discovered that some choices are easier in hindsight than they are in the moment. Life often presents options without clear outcomes, leaving only instincts, values, and courage to guide the way. I remember deciding whether to confront a misunderstanding with a close friend or remain silent. Fear of conflict tempted me to retreat, but listening to my instincts, I chose honest communication. The conversation was difficult, but it deepened our bond and taught me that courageous choices often create growth and connection.

Choices also shape self-identity. I realized that by consciously choosing who I wanted to be, how I wanted to act, and what I wanted to pursue, I was slowly sculpting my own identity. Each decision reflected my priorities, values, and aspirations. I understood that indecision or passive acceptance often allows external forces to define who we are. Choosing consciously is a declaration of agency, autonomy, and self-respect.

I recall a time when I was torn between two hobbies—one popular among my friends, the other deeply personal and meaningful. External pressure urged me toward popularity, but my heart leaned toward authenticity. Choosing the path that resonated with me not only brought joy but also strengthened my sense of self. Choices that align with personal values nourish fulfillment, while those based on external expectations often lead to regret.

Another dimension of choice is the balance between patience and action. I noticed that impulsive decisions, while sometimes exciting, often led to mistakes or stress. On the other hand, overthinking can paralyze. I began learning when to act decisively and when to wait, understanding that timing is as crucial as the choice itself. Wisdom lies not only in what we choose but also in when and how we choose.

Choices are often intertwined with fear. Fear of failure, rejection, judgment, or loss can cloud judgment and freeze action. I recall applying for a leadership role I secretly desired but feared I wasn't capable of handling. Every thought whispered doubt, yet the desire to challenge myself and learn prevailed. I leaped, and although the path was difficult, I discovered hidden strengths and abilities. Courage and choice go hand in hand, especially when fear is present.

I realized that some choices require letting go. Letting go of expectations, attachments, or comfort zones is a choice that often leads to growth. I remember deciding to step away from a group project where my contributions were undervalued, despite the fear of judgment or criticism. The choice allowed me to redirect energy toward opportunities where my efforts mattered. Choosing to let go is as powerful as choosing to hold on.

Choices also affect relationships. Choosing empathy over reaction, listening over arguing, or forgiveness over resentment can transform connections. I noticed that intentional decisions in relationships foster trust, understanding, and respect. I began observing patterns: relationships thrived when nurtured with conscious choices rather than left to chance. The quality of relationships often reflects the choices we make daily.

I learned that ethical choices matter deeply. In school and social settings, I faced situations where shortcuts, deception, or convenience tempted me. I realized that even minor compromises in integrity erode self-respect over time. I chose honesty, even when it was difficult, and gradually, trust and credibility became natural companions. Ethical decision-making strengthens character and self-belief.

The Power of Choices

Another lesson is that choices shape emotional resilience. Life is unpredictable, and no decision guarantees a smooth journey. Mistakes, failures, or unexpected outcomes are inevitable. By choosing intentionally and accepting responsibility, I cultivated resilience, learning to adapt, recover, and grow rather than succumb to regret or blame. Every choice, even imperfect, becomes a lesson and a step forward.

I noticed that reflection enhances the quality of choices. Pausing to consider long-term impact, values, and priorities prevents impulsive actions. I started journaling before making significant decisions, listing potential outcomes, risks, and how they align with my personal goals. This practice not only clarified options but strengthened confidence in decision-making. Reflection turns choices into deliberate acts rather than reactions to circumstance.

I also realized that some choices

require negotiation between desire and practicality. Balancing dreams with responsibility, ambition with limitations, and passion with resources is challenging but essential. I recall wanting to pursue multiple creative projects simultaneously while fulfilling my academic commitments. Strategic planning, prioritization, and compromise allowed me to follow both passion and responsibility. Effective choices often require flexibility, strategy, and foresight.

Choices can also inspire others. When I witnessed peers making bold, principled decisions, it motivated me to act with courage and authenticity. Conversely, my choices sometimes had a positive influence on others, whether by modeling integrity, determination, or self-respect. I understood that choices extend beyond personal impact, shaping communities, relationships, and culture.

I discovered that choosing consistently

builds habits and identity. Daily decisions—how to respond to challenges, how to invest time, how to treat others—accumulate into patterns that define life. I observed that discipline and intentionality in small choices often outweigh occasional grand decisions.

I also realized that patience and acceptance are necessary when outcomes are uncertain. Not every decision yields immediate results. I remember choosing to study diligently for a competition, unsure of success. The results were delayed, but persistence and belief in my choice eventually led to achievement. Patience honors the process, while action honors intention.

Choices intersect with courage, reflection, self-awareness, and integrity. By embracing this interconnectedness, I learned to navigate life with intention, clarity, and authenticity. Decisions became empowering rather than burdensome, and the weight of responsibility transformed into a sense of freedom. I understood that to choose consciously is to claim ownership of life itself.

I also observed that some choices require risk. Choosing comfort over challenge may feel safe, but it limits growth. I remember volunteering for a leadership role that demanded skills I had yet to master. The choice was intimidating, but the experience taught me adaptability, creativity, and resilience. Courageous risk-taking, I realized, magnifies the potential of every choice.

Ultimately, I realized that self-trust is crucial in decision-making. Doubt is inevitable, but by grounding choices in values, reflection, and intuition, I strengthened confidence and reduced regret. Even when outcomes were unexpected, the knowledge that I had chosen intentionally provided peace, clarity, and strength. The power of choice lies not only in the results but also in the integrity and awareness that guide the decision.

Choices, small and large, visible and invisible, define life's trajectory. Each decision carries potential for growth, connection, and self-discovery. By choosing consciously, courageously, and thoughtfully, we shape not only outcomes but also who we are, how we relate, and the life we create.

Chapter 30

The Journey Ahead

"The path forward is yours; walk it with courage and authenticity."

The journey ahead is an unknown landscape, filled with possibilities, challenges, and opportunities waiting to be discovered. Standing at the edge of the familiar and peering into what lies beyond, I feel a mixture of excitement, anticipation, and the weight of responsibility. Life does not offer a map with clear directions;

it provides choices, lessons, and experiences, and it is up to us to navigate the path with courage, clarity, and authenticity.

I have spent years observing, reflecting, and learning about myself and the world around me. I've seen how small decisions accumulate into patterns that define character, how moments of silence reveal truths that are unseen in the noise, and how courage, self-belief, and intentional choices shape the trajectory of life. Each experience, failure, success, and reflection has been a stepping stone leading to this point–a moment to look forward rather than backward.

I remember the first time I faced uncertainty that felt larger than anything I had experienced before. I was about to embark on a project that would challenge every skill and confidence I had accumulated. Fear pressed against me, whispering doubts, "What if you fail? What if you aren't enough?" But I realized that the journey ahead is not meant to be a path of comfort—it is a path of growth. Every challenge, every obstacle, and every triumph is part of the unfolding story, a story that only I can write. Life moves forward when we embrace the unknown with courage rather than recoil from it. The journey ahead is also a journey of self-discovery. Each decision, each encounter, and each experience reveals layers of personality, values, and desires previously hidden. I've learned that the more deeply I know myself, the more intentional my choices become. I understand that the journey ahead requires curiosity, introspection, and the willingness to face not only the world but also the truths within. Self-awareness is both a compass and a guide, directing steps through uncertainty.

I have learned that resilience will be essential on this journey. Life is unpredictable; setbacks are inevitable, and circumstances often challenge the limits of patience, creativity, and perseverance. I remember failing at something I had worked tirelessly for—the disappointment was crushing. Still, reflection revealed that the experience was not a dead end but a lesson in adaptation and persistence. The journey ahead will demand resilience, not only in response to failure but in embracing the continuous process of learning and evolving.

Connection and relationships will be another defining part of the path forward. I have come to realize that no journey is truly solitary. The people we encounter, support, and collaborate with influence the course of our lives. Friends, mentors, and even casual acquaintances offer perspectives, inspiration, and opportunities for growth. Choosing whom to trust, when to open up, and when to support others is part of navigating the journey wisely. Relationships are not distractions but catalysts for learning, compassion, and shared strength.

The journey ahead also requires embracing change. Nothing in life remains static. Opportunities, challenges, and circumstances constantly evolve, and the ability to adapt without compromising integrity is a vital skill. I have witnessed how resisting change often magnifies difficulty, whereas flexibility allows growth and transformation. Embracing change with awareness, courage, and intentionality ensures that each step forward contributes to the person I aspire to become.

Reflection will remain a constant companion. Pausing to consider lessons learned, values clarified, and progress made allows recalibration when needed. I remember moments when I rushed forward without consideration, only to realize that deliberate reflection would have prevented unnecessary mistakes. The journey ahead demands a balance between action and contemplation, between courage and discernment, between ambition and patience. Reflection ensures that movement is purposeful rather than hasty.

I have also learned that authenticity will guide the journey. Pretending to be someone else, conforming to expectations, or hiding true feelings may seem protective, but ultimately stifles growth. The journey ahead will reward those who are honest, courageous, and genuinely self-expressive. By staying true to values, passions, and vision, I can navigate challenges confidently, even when others doubt or misunderstand. Authenticity becomes a shield, compass, and source of inner strength.

Another insight is that learning is a lifelong process. The journey ahead is a continuous classroom, presenting opportunities to acquire knowledge, wisdom, and skill. Every interaction, experience, and challenge offers a lesson if I remain observant, curious, and open-minded. I have learned to embrace humility in my learning, acknowledging gaps without shame and proactively seeking growth. The willingness to learn will transform the journey from mere passage through time into a meaningful adventure.

I also recognize that the journey ahead will demand courage in choices. Fear will always be present—fear of failure, judgment, or uncertainty. Yet, the path forward is defined not by the absence of fear but by the courage to act despite it. Each decision will have consequences, and each action will carry weight. By aligning my choices with my values and purpose, I can navigate with confidence, knowing that even mistakes contribute to my growth. Courage in decision-making illuminates the path in darkness.

The journey ahead is also a journey of contribution. Life is not only about personal growth but also about impact—how my actions, words, and presence influence others. I have seen how small gestures of empathy, guidance, and support ripple outward, touching lives in ways that are often unseen and unappreciated. The choices I make, the efforts I invest, and the courage I display will shape not only my story but also the stories of those I encounter. Purposeful contribution amplifies the meaning of the journey.

I have learned that the journey ahead requires patience. Progress is rarely linear, and the unfolding of dreams, skills, and opportunities often takes time to develop. I remember waiting for results after months of effort, feeling anxious, restless, and uncertain. Patience, combined with sustained action, proved vital. I realized that trusting the process and pacing oneself is as crucial as ambition and effort.

Intuition will guide me as much as logic. I have found that inner wisdom often perceives nuances beyond rational calculation. The journey ahead will require listening closely to instincts, feelings, and subtle signals, integrating them with deliberate thought. Balancing intuition with strategy allows navigation with clarity, awareness, and effectiveness. Intuition becomes a trusted ally in uncertainty.

I also recognize that failures along the journey will be inevitable and valuable. Each setback will teach valuable lessons, highlight resilience, and reveal strengths that were previously unnoticed. I have learned that failure is not the end but a pivot—a chance to recalibrate, adapt, and improve. The journey ahead will be shaped not by avoiding failure, but by the courage to embrace it and learn from it. Failure can be transformed into fuel when approached with perspective and persistence.

Creativity and innovation will shape the path forward. By thinking boldly, experimenting freely, and embracing curiosity, I can craft innovative solutions, explore new possibilities, and make the journey both exciting and fulfilling. I have learned that risk-taking, informed exploration, and imaginative thinking transform ordinary paths into remarkable adventures. Creativity breathes life into the journey ahead.

I realize that self-care and balance are essential. The journey ahead is long, and the energy, focus, and emotional resilience required demand attention to health, rest, and personal well-being. Overcommitment, neglect, or burnout can obscure vision and hinder progress. I have learned to honor boundaries, listen to needs, and cultivate habits that sustain energy, focus, and joy. Self-care is not an indulgence, but rather preparation for meaningful action.

I also recognize that gratitude will illuminate the journey. Appreciating progress, relationships, opportunities, and lessons cultivates optimism, resilience, and a sense of contentment. Reflection on achievements and acknowledgment of support strengthen confidence and perspective.

Gratitude turns ordinary moments into

milestones and challenges into growth opportunities.

The journey ahead is ultimately a testament to growth, courage, and self-determination. Each chapter of life—past, present, and future—contributes to an evolving narrative. I have learned to embrace uncertainty with faith in my abilities, a curiosity for exploration, and a commitment to my values. I step forward aware that the path will be imperfect, demanding, and unpredictable, yet filled with possibility, learning, and connection.

As I stand at this threshold, I realize that the journey ahead is not a destination to reach but a process to embrace. It is defined not solely by accomplishments but by choices, courage, reflection, authenticity, and resilience. I am prepared to navigate with awareness, to act with intention, and to live fully in each moment, knowing that the story of life is shaped not by waiting for perfection but by embracing every step with purpose and presence.

The journey ahead belongs to those willing to move with courage, curiosity, and conviction. I choose to walk it boldly, thoughtfully, and authentically, embracing every twist, challenge, and opportunity. Life is both teacher and canvas, and I am ready to create, learn, and grow—one choice, one step, one moment at a time.

Conclusion

The journey of life is full of choices, lessons, and moments that shape who we are. What you have read in these pages is a reflection of my own experiences, thoughts, and reflections—a small guide for anyone navigating the path of self-discovery and growth.

I hope these stories inspire you to embrace your own journey with courage, curiosity, and authenticity. Life will always present challenges, moments of doubt, and unexpected turns, but every experience is an opportunity to learn, grow, and become stronger.

Remember, the power to shape your journey lies within you—in your choices, your reflections, and your courage to stay true to yourself. Each step, each decision, and each moment of honesty adds to the story of who you are becoming.

This book is meant to accompany you as you explore, reflect, and grow—a reminder that your journey is unique, valuable, and worth living fully. Carry these lessons with you, and step forward with confidence, authenticity, and an open heart.

Letter from the Author

Dear Reader,

I wanted to take a moment to speak to you personally before you begin this journey through Becoming Real: A Journey Through Courage and Self-Discovery. This book comes from my heart—from the moments I felt too different, too raw, or too real for the world around me. I wrote it not to teach, but to share, to connect, and to remind anyone who has ever felt out of place that they are not alone.

Every page is a piece of my journey, a reflection of the courage it takes to stay true to yourself in a world that often asks you to hide. If you resonate, if a part of this resonates with your soul, then this book has found its purpose. It is not for everyone—it is for those brave enough to be real.

Thank you for opening it, and thank you for daring to feel deeply with me.

With love and truth,
Shivangi Gupta

About the Author

Shivangi Gupta, born on 5th November 2010 in India, Uttar Pradesh, is a young writer who gives voice to the unspoken emotions and truths of her generation. Her writing combines raw honesty, emotional depth, and empowering reflections, capturing the experiences of those who feel deeply, think profoundly, and refuse to conform.

Through "Not for Everyone", Shivangi explores the challenges of self-discovery, authenticity, relationships, and personal growth in a world that constantly demands conformity. Her words resonate with anyone navigating the complex journey of being unapologetically themselves, offering insights, strength, and inspiration without ever coming across as preachy.

Shivangi writes for those who have felt misunderstood, underestimated, or overlooked—for those learning that being real is a choice worth making, even if it means not being for everyone.